Creating new opportunities re k/
Life Flywheel model, Ollie Hen 'd
to make bold changes in your c: ar
ideas with the world.

Daniel I g
author of ... .. u w c/ uj regret, When, and Drive

We all know that the old three-stage life course of full-time education, full-time work and full-time retirement is not fit for purpose. But we also know that to make the changes to a more flexible and adaptive multi-stage life, we need to be bold and courageous. In this inspiring book, Henderson shows the foundations for this courage and shares the stories of those who have created momentum and energy in their working life.

Lynda Gratton, author of *Redesigning Work,*
Professor of Management Practice at London Business School

Ollie is an important and empathetic voice in the conversation around the future of work. His book will help us all navigate a better way to work and live.

Annie Auerbach, author of *FLEX, Reinventing*
Work for a Smarter and Happier Life

Work and leisure have become a false dichotomy. As Ollie Henderson shows using the superb Flywheel metaphor, done right, each can make you better at the other.

Rory Sutherland, Vice-Chairman of Ogilvy,
author of *Alchemy: The Surprising Power of*
Ideas That Don't Make Sense

Ollie's excellent book will show you the practical techniques of reimagining your life and career and reveals how much better things could be for you, if you can adopt his hard-earned wisdom.

Damian Hughes, host of *The High Performance*
podcast and author of *High Performance* and *Liquid Thinker*

Ollie Henderson gives you the tools to create a legendary career by embracing being different, harnessing your creativity and building a system to share your ideas. Forget chasing work/life balance and build a Work/Life Flywheel instead.

Christopher Lochhead, 11 x #1 bestselling
author of *Category Pirates*, *Play Bigger* and *Niche Down*

Work/Life Flywheel puts to bed the notion that our work-life balance is an either/or trade off: the two move in tandem, and this book helps us find that binding rhythm.

Will Page, author of *Tarzan Economics* and
former Chief Economist of Spotify

Work/Life Flywheel offers honest and practical advice from accomplished industry mavens coupled with candid reflections on their real experiences when trying to recreate themselves professionally and personally. A must-read for anyone looking to make bold changes in their career and at home.

Emily Balcetis, author of *Clearer, Closer, Better:
How Successful People See the World*,
Associate Professor of Psychology at New York University

Ollie and I have similar stories: burned-out agency owners who started writing online and experienced life-changing results. If this sounds like you too (whether you're an entrepreneur or a high-achieving, exhausted employee), then you'll feel right at home reading this book.

Nicolas Cole, 8 x author and captain of *Ship 30 for 30*

If you want to redefine your life and work relationship, get connected to the wisdom inside *Work/Life Flywheel*.

Shaun Tomson, Surfing World Champion
and author of *The Code: The Power of "I Will"*

If you want to reimagine what's possible in the worlds of work and life beyond work, then this book will give your brain, thought processes and imagination a fascinating and exhilarating workout to help you develop fresh thinking about how to create the best future for you.

Cath Bishop, Olympic rowing medallist,
former diplomat, leadership coach, and author of *The Long Win*

In *Work/Life Flywheel*, Henderson deftly combines decades of wisdom to create a compelling framework for how we think about work and life in today's complex world. Using insights gleaned from academic research, business leaders, personal anecdotes, and his own life, Henderson provides a conversational and practical approach to stepping out of your routines, creatively considering a new way of approaching work and life, and taking practical steps to make it happen. If you're ready for change but aren't sure where to begin, this book is a great place to start!

Alyssa Westring, co-author of *Parents Who Lead*,
Chair of the Department of Management
and Entrepreneurship at DePaul University

Ollie Henderson offers a timely and perceptive critique of the never-ending pursuit of work/life balance, and suggests a better way to build momentum in our personal and professional lives.

Alex Hutchinson, author of *Endure: Mind, Body, and
the Curiously Elastic Limits of Human Performance*

With the right mindset and systems, you can make positive changes in your career. Ollie Henderson's *Work/Life Flywheel* gives you the tools and motivation to develop both, creating the momentum you need to maximise your potential and succeed in the new world of work.

Justin Welsh, entrepreneur, investor, and SaaS advisor

The world is changing fast, and life can be short – so we might as well start making it meaningful, today. This book provides a superbly pragmatic and useful take on how we can reimagine our career and life. A book worth reading and an approach worth taking.

Dr Christian Busch, bestselling author of
*The Serendipity Mindset: The Art and Science of
Creating Good Luck*, and professor, New York University

As people are beginning to reimagine work and reconsider their careers, *Work/Life Flywheel* is a brilliant resource to help you get started in redesigning your work/life.

Elizabeth Akanbi-Ogabi, author of *Side Hustle in Progress*

Ollie Henderson's *Work/Life Flywheel* offers the practical tools to redesign your work and reimagine the career of your dreams. Whether you're amid a big pivot or you're looking for a healthy dose of inspiration to find what your next chapter will hold, the tangible insights and success stories in *Work/Life Flywheel* will help harness your mindset, spark your creativity, and lead to substantial breakthroughs for harmony and alignment in both your personal and professional life.

Kathrin Hamm, CEO of Bearaby

There isn't a person out there that hasn't thought about radically reinventing work and life. What's been missing is an accessible guidebook to transform desire-to-action, and action-to-outcome. Ollie Henderson's *Work/Life Flywheel* sketches out a framework for thinking about transformation, bringing the lessons to life with his own personal journey, along with expert insight from industry figures who have themselves gone on idiosyncratic paths to successful unconventional futures. Fantastic read, and essential for anyone thinking about career change.

Hung Lee, Curator, Recruiting Brainfood

Life is a continuous learning journey with feedback loops along the way to help us reflect and adapt where appropriate. The *Work/Life Flywheel* is a much-needed read after the world has experienced a pandemic that puts the harmony of our work and personal lives in question.

Andy Ayim MBE, founder of Angel Investing School

Henderson provides clear direction and practical steps to help you find the work/life harmony that you richly deserve. The Flywheel's 6 building blocks offer an easy to follow guide for your journey.

Marc Effron, author of *8 Steps to High Performance* and President of The Talent Strategy Group

WORK/LIFE FLYWHEEL

Harness the work revolution and
reimagine your career without fear

OLLIE HENDERSON

First published in Great Britain by Practical Inspiration Publishing, 2023

ISBN   9781788603515 (print)
        9781788603539 (epub)
        9781788603522 (mobi)

Want to bulk-buy copies of this book for your team and colleagues? We can introduce case studies, customize the content and co-brand *Work/Life Flywheel* to suit your business's needs.

Please email info@practicalinspiration.com for more details.

To Carly, Theo, Emmie & Asa

Contents

Foreword

One warm summer morning, a woman spotted the great artist Pablo Picasso walking through a market in Provence. She pursued him and pulled out a piece of paper.

'Mr Picasso,' she said excitedly, 'I'm a big fan. Please, could you do a little drawing for me?'

Picasso happily complied and quickly drew a sketch for her on the scrap of paper. As he handed it back, he smiled, then told her to 'take care of it. That will be worth a million dollars one day.'

The woman looked flustered and said, 'but it only took you thirty seconds to do it'.

Picasso laughed, 'but it has taken me thirty years to be able to do it in thirty seconds'.

This – possibly apocryphal – tale is a great place to introduce you to this book and the ideas within it.

Ollie's excellent book will show you the practical techniques of reimagining your life and career and reveals how much better things could be for you, if you can adopt his hard-earned wisdom.

The great news is this can be taught, and the even better news is that, unlike Picasso, it will not take you 30 years to acquire the knowledge (unless you are an exceptionally slow reader).

So, whether you want to improve your own life, your relationships, or your ambitions, let this wonderful book be your guide.

Professor Damian Hughes

Introduction:
The big pivot

MY STORY

It's January 2020, and I've just negotiated my exit from the digital agency I founded and have been running for over ten years.

After a decade in advertising and media, I'm ready for a fresh challenge, but I'll admit, I have no idea what. The money I've made has bought me a little time, but given my hefty monthly mortgage payments and an ever-expanding family (three kids and counting), I reckon I've got about six months before I have to be earning again. I'm pretty sure that when you pivot your career, you're supposed to have a clearer plan, but I figure if I take some time off to relax and rejuvenate, before too long I can have a new business up and running that will launch me back into the world full of vim and vigour.

If only it were that straightforward.

Two months later, the world is in lockdown and COVID-19 has thrown not just my plans but those of almost every business in the world up in the air. Not ideal timing.

Feeling the pressure to work out a plan of action, I take the advice of a friend who'd been through a similar experience a few years before (minus the global pandemic). After exiting his first business, he built another start-up, before, this time, selling to a larger marketing services group. He wishes he'd documented his journey setting that business up, capturing the emotions and breakthroughs he'd experienced along the way, and suggests I write about the process I'm going through. Memories fade all too quickly.

High up on my list of priorities is rethinking my relationship with work.

For ten years, I've been anxious that I'm neither spending enough time at work nor at home. I've never been able to achieve the perfect balance. After burning out a few times, I know something has to change, although this doesn't involve getting a regular job. I've been my own boss for too long.

Whatever comes next, I'm determined to be in control of my own destiny.

I soon discover that whether you're making a sideways step in a familiar industry, going solo as a freelancer, or setting up a new business, there are so many variables to consider when going through a career transition and it can quickly become overwhelming. If you have dependants – whether a partner, kids, or other family members – to support, then not only do you have the pressure of making the 'right' decision in this next critical stage of your career, you have to make sure you can pay the bills while you do it.

Add the increasing pressure of achieving the *perfect* work/life balance, and you can understand why it puts most people off and how they end up stuck in jobs they hate.

Stepping back from the day-to-day pressures of running a company, it hasn't taken long to realize that the concept of work/life balance is a myth. While it's a metaphor used with well-meaning intentions, in reality it represents something unattainable – a perfect equilibrium between the time you spend at work and the rest of your life.

The more I speak with others and reflect on the future, the clearer three things become:

1. I'm not the only person attempting to reimagine my career while juggling the pleasures and pressures of a young family.
2. The ability to clearly communicate ideas will only get more important in the future, so I need to get over my reluctance to 'put myself out there' and start sharing mine.
3. Aspiring for work/life balance is not helping me achieve my goals and I need a new approach.

I start considering what I can do to help others, like me, feel less like they're failing to live up to unrealistic expectations.

How can I help people think differently about the relationship between their work and personal lives?

Is it possible to develop a model that others can use to reimagine their work/lives?

STARTING TO WRITE

As I explore these themes, I take what would before this point have been an unthinkable step of publishing my writing online – in public! As someone who avoids this at all costs, it's a significant move, but I press the publish button in the spirit of new beginnings. Plus, I figure no one will read it anyway.

Two weeks later, I've had over 20 direct messages from people who'd read the honest accounts of my ongoing thought process, which is enough to keep me going.

With COVID-19 fundamentally rearranging the boundaries between our work and personal lives, many others seem to relate to my experience. I decide to start a newsletter to explore this more, and have hundreds of subscribers within a couple of days. When momentum builds, sometimes you have to just let it carry you.

A few months later, not only have I grown to love the process of writing, but it's also creating new opportunities. People are even introducing me as an expert on the future of work. I just nod.

Fast forward a couple of years and I've…

- Spent thousands of hours understanding what dynamics drive people's decision-making while undertaking an often scary-seeming career pivot.
- Interviewed world champion sportspeople, bestselling authors and visionary entrepreneurs across more than 100 episodes of my Top 10 Careers podcast, *Future Work/Life*.
- Launched a fast-growing newsletter, and grown a global community interested in the future of work.

- Gathered quantitative survey data from over 4,000 people and had countless one-to-one conversations with people reimagining their careers.

As I spoke to more and more successful people from the world of business and explored work/life design with leading experts in subjects as varied as psychology, sport, behavioural science, artificial intelligence, and the arts, a model emerged.

While no single story was the same, I kept spotting the same characteristics and patterns of behaviour among those who've successfully navigated these transitions. They've developed a positive and complementary relationship between their work and personal lives that allows them to keep one foot in the present and one in the future – a Work/Life Flywheel.

THE WORK/LIFE FLYWHEEL

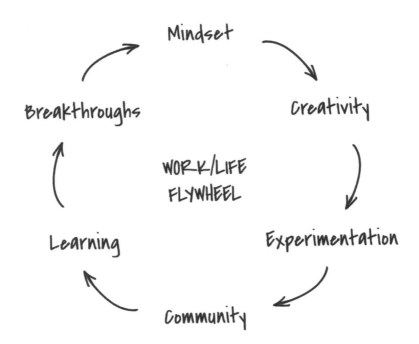

The Work/Life Flywheel is a model which will give you the confidence to create your expert niche and tell the story about why it matters, propelling you forward into the next phase of your career.

Adapting the Flywheel to reflect your motivations, personality, and circumstances will empower you to harness the revolutionary changes happening in the world of work and to carve out your unique place within it. You'll find it continuously sparks ideas and provokes new possibilities, creating growth opportunities that give you the forward impetus you need to succeed and be happy.

While achieving significant changes won't happen overnight, stacking small wins on top of one another will enable you to build a complementary relationship between your work and personal life.

We'll uncover how to effectively combine physical activity with rest and recovery to supercharge your creativity. We'll examine why following your curiosity relies upon an openness to experimentation and why the inevitable failures help deepen understanding and accelerate our learning. We'll also break down how incorporating a creative approach into every aspect of your work/life leads to new relationships, access to communities of like-minded folk, and helps you build the confidence to do your thinking in public.

As I share real-world examples of people who started their new adventures with trepidation, you'll begin to recognize the Flywheel in their work/life design.

Rather than view each part of the model – mindset, creativity, experimentation, community, learning and breakthroughs – in isolation, you'll observe how they create a virtuous circle. The habits you build will allow you to embrace uncertainty and take control of your future by providing the momentum to continue creating and building.

Combining the stories of people who have walked the path you're on with the very best evidence-based research, I'll give you the tools to reimagine your career without fear.

You'll get the most value out of reading the book in the order I've written it, but you can easily return to each chapter for actionable advice if you're stuck at any stage. For example, if you need to refine your goal-setting, you can dig back into Chapter 8. Or, if you find that although you've started your Flywheel spinning, you're not making as much progress as you'd like in building your network, you can revisit Chapter 16.

Finally, you'll notice that the stories I share could fit comfortably into several other parts of the book. That's the point. Your work/life isn't neatly divided into distinct parts. It's messy and overlapping. Some parts gel nicely and others you have to work harder on. The benefits of the Work/Life Flywheel lie in how all the components work together to create something greater than the sum of their parts. Used as a lens through which to prioritize how to spend your time and energy, the results are profound and life-changing.

Life and work are a series of challenges to overcome and opportunities to discover. The Work/Life Flywheel gives you a proven approach to do this successfully, time after time.

Let's get started.

THE WORK
REVOLUTION

1

Harness the work revolution

We've all heard the phrase:

With great change, comes great opportunity.

The question is, what are you going to do about it?

In 2004, MIT graduate Salman Khan had just graduated from his MBA class at Harvard when he agreed to remotely tutor his young cousin, who was struggling with her high school maths work. Pretty quickly, word got out in the family that Sal was offering free sessions, and before too long, he no longer had the spare time to do them one-to-one. On their suggestion, he started recording sessions onto YouTube, meaning they could view them at their leisure.

By 2009, the Khan Academy was founded, with a mission to 'provide a free, world-class education for anyone, anywhere'.

While the Khan Academy may not have been the first case of what became known as 'flipped education', it was the example that brought the term into public consciousness. Educators learned that students were more engaged when they could control their learning pace when studying at home, whether reading or using on-demand video.

They would then spend their time in class on problem-solving and discussion, with the teacher acting as a facilitator and coach.

Sound familiar?

The world of work, like education before it, has now been turned upside down.

Allison Baum Gates is a venture capitalist and was one of my first guests on the *Future Work/Life* podcast. As one of the early hires at General Assembly, another pioneer of online education, Allison was ahead of the curve in realizing how technology would enable a more personalized approach in the workplace. In 2019, she wrote about why we've entered the 'flipped workplace' era, in which organizations could leverage the benefits of focused time away from the office while coming together, when required, for collaboration and opportunities for spontaneity and serendipity.

> Productive individual work is done outside of the office, on your own time, in your own place, at your own pace. Consequently, the office transforms into a space purely dedicated to meeting people, asking questions, brainstorming, and making unexpected connections. Liberated from enforcement of time-based productivity, managers don't need to be babysitters. Instead they are coaches, enablers, and facilitators focused on unlocking each employee's unique value to the entire organization.[1]

Given what we know now about what's become universally known as 'hybrid work', this description looks prescient.

Yet you could easily argue that we've skipped the 'flipped workplace' entirely. Only a few years after remote working was a peculiarity reserved for a handful of tech businesses, millions of people worldwide will never return to the office. The relationship between their work and personal lives has fundamentally changed.

We're in the middle of the greatest work/life transition ever.

---

[1] https://qz.com/work/1551999/the-benefits-of-flipped-workplaces-include-protection-from-ai/

WHERE, WHEN, HOW AND WHY?

While the first encounter many of us had with this emerging work revolution was a change in *where* we worked, we soon spotted the opportunity to rethink other dimensions of our work/lives.

- If we're no longer constrained to the office, how about we reconsider *when* and *how* we work too?
- Could we monetize our skills and experience outside a conventional 9–5 job and 'go it alone'?

The number of people moving into freelance careers has been on the rise since the Great Recession of 2007 to 2009, but since 2020 the rate of new company registrations in the UK and USA has accelerated. A new wave of entrepreneurship has emerged as so many have explored the benefits of becoming free agents for the first time. And yet, perhaps the most profound trend to emerge is a collective reassessment of our priorities in work and life.

As the COVID-19 pandemic put our lives on temporary hold, we started wondering:

- Why are we wasting time commuting into an office *every day*?
- Why are we spending so much time in meetings?
- Why the hell do we do what we do anyway?!

Alongside the pent-up demand that provoked what became known as the 'Great Resignation' in the second half of 2021, survey data consistently showed that purpose was now a vital consideration as candidates contemplated which company they should join. Among Generation Z – the youngest portion of working adults – in particular, whether or not their prospective employer's values aligned with theirs became more significant than the salary on offer.[2]

The work revolution is empowering us to look for something more than just money and status.

---

[2] www.ey.com/en_us/news/2021/11/ey-releases-gen-z-survey-revealing-businesses-must-rethink-their-plan-z

HOW CAN WE REDESIGN WORK?

Lynda Gratton, Professor at London Business School, is one of the world's leading experts on organizational behaviour and wrote the definitive book on how firms are *Redesigning Work*.

She explained to me that after the initial retreat to homes at the beginning of the pandemic, the pressure for workplace change came directly from employees. As people quickly adapted to the circumstances forced upon them, they soon recognized the benefits of working more flexibly, pushing them to force employers to behave differently, starting with how we design jobs and where and when we're most productive. And it has not stopped there. The rebalancing of power between businesses and individuals has also opened our eyes to new possibilities.

Millions are now weighing up whether to pursue an alternative path to traditional employment.

WHAT'S CHANGING?

Tom Haak runs the HR Trend Institute and spends much of his time analysing trends in organizational design, people and workplace culture so we don't have to.

Every year, his trends report shapes the strategies of businesses around the world and if you want a glimpse into the dynamics influencing how we design jobs, he's your man. During the uncertainty of two years of locking down, he tracked businesses in reactive mode, adapting on the fly to the fast-changing and unprecedented circumstances. But as we've begun to emerge from this period, the emphasis has moved to transformation – a substantial and ongoing evolution.

Tom told me that the pandemic had proven an accelerant to many existing work trends, as in so many other walks of life.

One of the most prominent is the need for organizations to become more flexible in how they think about the make-up of their workforce. According to a 2021 McKinsey report,[3] the most important factors

---

[3] www.mckinsey.com/business-functions/people-and-organizational-performance/our-insights/great-attrition-or-great-attraction-the-choice-is-yours

behind people making decisions about moving roles included being valued by your manager, feeling a sense of belonging, the potential for advancement, and having a flexible work schedule. However, the best talent wasn't just jumping from one employer to another. An increasing number decided to leave full-time employment entirely and 'go it alone'.

While hiring consultants and freelancers is nothing new, the difference this time is the scale at which this new 'flexible' workforce is growing.

WHY IS THIS HAPPENING?

There's a reason I used that word, 'flexible'.

You don't have to wait for your employer to create an enlightened work policy when you work for yourself. Aside from pressing client meetings, you're in charge of what time you get out of bed in the morning, how frequently you exercise, and whether you take that lunchtime nap. However, flexibility in when and how you work isn't the only thing at play. A desire for more autonomy also applies to choosing which clients you work for and what you do for them.

And, of course, financial considerations are significant.

Enabled by technology and talent-matching platforms, the chance to maximize your value by going direct to clients and creating greater long-term security is enough for many people to initially offset the risk of sometimes patchy revenue.

Sounds great, right?

Yes. However, as well as the many positives, too many freelancers still experience a sense of 'feast or famine'. They're turning work away at some points, while at others it feels like they're scrabbling around for enough to pay the bills.

If this sounds like you, don't worry. With a mindset shift and the right strategy, you can shift from a freelancer to a solopreneur, with a consistent stream of opportunities and a more diverse portfolio of work, including creating recurring revenue and products that produce passive income.

Later in the book, we'll explore how taking a creative and experimental approach to your work will generate new ways of positioning your expertise, which you can then monetize more effectively by cultivating a community.

WHAT DOES IT MEAN FOR BUSINESSES?

None of this would be possible if there wasn't sufficient demand for flexible workers.

For a services business, like a marketing agency, for example, that might mean rapidly deploying expert teams in response to a client brief. The alternative would either be an often lengthy recruitment process followed by a long notice period, or upskilling an existing employee. By the time you've done all of this, the urgent need, and the opportunity, may have passed.

The finances can work out for both parties too.

While an individual can leverage their unique experience and expertise to increase their earnings potential, businesses can access high-calibre, specialized talent on a needs-only basis. Day rates or retainer fees may, at first glance, look expensive compared to a salary, but relative to the time required to deliver the goods, the picture often looks very different.

In the future, organizations will become far more fluid, both in the ways employees work – through flexible time and location – and in the make-up of the workforce.

Tim Oldman, CEO of workplace insights firm Leesman, explained that their research showed clearly that the businesses that thrived during the uncertain and unpredictable pandemic period were those who responded flexibly and creatively. Not just in terms of how they reorientated their people to either office or home-based working, but also how they thought about job design. For example, if the location and environment you're working in fundamentally change, so should the expectations on how you *do* your job, including the time you spend on 'heads-down' compared to collaborative work.

Previously, people assumed that the 'knowledge economy' was not suited to a decentralized model like this, for a few key reasons, often related to workplace culture or performance management concerns.

'You can't create a great culture with a bunch of temporary and remote staff', they'd say.

And when it comes to flexible workers like freelancers and contractors, unimaginative leaders would claim that:

'If they're not full time, they're not as invested in the business's success.'

Not any more.

Thankfully, we've learned that there's more than one way to skin a cat.

Over the coming years, we'll see ever increasing numbers of 'knowledge workers' bringing their skills and expertise to businesses, and sometimes they may even do so for more than one business at a time. Rather than see this as a conflict of interests, we'll reframe it as a chance to capitalize on the unique knowledge and insights they gain from solving business problems across diverse categories.

While the changing dynamics of the workforce appear complex, they present tremendous possibilities for everyone concerned.

A competitive advantage exists for organizations that recognize the opportunity and choose to embrace it. Meanwhile, a new generation of solopreneurs and entrepreneurs will have more control over their futures and can maximize their value in the market.

How would you design your work/life if you could start from scratch?

What do you prioritize most – security, flexibility, money, or variety?

How can you take advantage of the work revolution to make big changes in your career?

We'll explore the answers to all these questions over the coming chapters, but first, let's dig into why now is the perfect time to make a transition.

SUMMARY

- Work has been flipped – we're now more likely to work at home than in an office.
- Younger generations care more that their values align with employers than how much money they earn.
- More people are becoming freelancers, solopreneurs and entrepreneurs than ever before.
- Technology and the internet are reducing the barriers to finding paid work.
- We're now reimagining job design based on dimensions like location and time.
- It will soon become normal to work for multiple businesses at a time.

2

Reimagine your career...

If it feels like your life has been thrown up in the air over the past few years, don't worry, you're not the only one.

Over several years, Bruce Feiler compiled more than a thousand hours of interviews to codify how we manage life transitions, meaning and purpose.[4] Rather than the traditional idea that life follows a straightforward, linear trajectory, he discovered that we actually experience a series of 'lifequakes' that fundamentally shift how we perceive our place in the world.

Lifequakes may be involuntary (such as a World War, a recession, or a partner leaving you) or voluntary (like quitting your job to start a new business or to travel around the world). We may experience these major upheavals personally or collectively, and we can characterize them by the questions that often arise. For example, questioning your purpose or exploring whether 'you're living the life you always dreamed of'. How we react to these events, however, is critical.

And this is where transitions come in.

Unlike lifequakes, which in some cases are out of our control, undergoing a transition is something we choose. Feiler describes this transitional process as having three parts, which are easily recognizable.

---

[4] Bruce Feiler, *Life Is in the Transitions: Mastering Change at Any Age*, Penguin, 2020.

1. 'The long goodbye', when we come to terms with leaving the old person behind.
2. 'The messy middle', in which we ditch some habits and acquire new ones.
3. 'The new beginning', in which we redefine our story to reflect a new direction.

THE INVOLUNTARY, COLLECTIVE TRANSITION

When I first came across Feiler's book, *Life is in the Transitions*, in May 2020, it touched a nerve.

I could see myself in the stories he told about the many thousands of people whose history he'd documented. More significantly, I wasn't alone. During the first few months of writing about my own experience of transitioning career, I lost count of the number of people who told me they were asking themselves the same existential questions.

Of course, given the circumstances, this wasn't a surprise.

Amidst a global pandemic – the very definition of a rare, involuntary and collective transition – the natural reaction was to reconsider what's important and reassess whether we were on track to achieving it.

The good news is that transitions work. They are an opportunity to break bad habits and adopt new, more positive ones. The trick is introducing these changes incrementally and establishing routines that help you make progress. Plus, we feel a sense of renewal and reinvention during a transitional period that (to continue the lyrical theme) helps reinvigorate and rejuvenate.

REINVENTING OURSELVES

If anyone understands the effects of a transition on our psychology and motivation, it's Beatrice Hackett.

After a decade working in financial services, charities, and for start-ups, she was disillusioned with her job and unsure what to do next. She began meeting with a life coach who asked her to focus on her values. What did she really care about?

The revelations that followed opened her eyes.

> It gave me huge insights into my work misery and how the values that matter to me were really misaligned with my work. For example, working in sales but not really being a person who values money. Valuing equality of opportunity while working in a very competitive environment. I love the space to choose and reflect, but in the corporate world I never found that.[5]

It had such a profound effect on Beatrice that she decided it was time to reassess her priorities and the direction her career would take. In particular, she reflected on how she might make a similarly significant impact on the lives of others to that her coach had on hers. The answer to her question of what to do next was staring her in the face.

She soon quit her job in the City, retrained as a coach, and now specializes in supporting others through career transitions.

A key component of her coaching methodology is how we think about our sense of identity. Very often, we define ourselves by the work we do. If you decide to pivot careers, you'll be doing something new and with that comes earning less money and, possibly, feeling like your status has reduced somehow. I experienced these feelings myself when I could no longer tell people I 'ran my own company'.

As Beatrice explained, that means taking a long, hard look in the mirror.

> First you have to acknowledge that you are in transition and give yourself space for – and I know these words aren't popular in the workplace – sadness, loss, and grief for letting go of what was. And then, when you spend time in this neutral zone where you actually don't know what's next, that's really challenging and it's the time we all need help and support, so that we have a new beginning and shift to something new.

---

[5] All quotations are taken from the *Future Work/Life* podcast unless indicated otherwise.

Once we've accepted that we're going through a transition, our focus can then switch to where we want to end up.

If you've already got a clear vision of your objective and the path you'll take to get there, you're very unusual but good for you! However, as I've learned over the past couple of years, there are always ways we can improve to increase our chances of success, so this book will help smooth the path ahead.

On the other hand, if you know that this is the time for a transition but have no idea how to get there, you're definitely in the right place. The Work/Life Flywheel is a model for exploring the next chapter of your career and will help you identify the incremental steps to progress.

First, let's focus on the wealth of opportunities that the work revolution is creating and consider how adapting our work/lives can help us carve out our niche within it.

PERSONALIZATION AT SCALE

We live in an era of personalization, certainly in our digital lives. So, why hasn't that filtered through to the way we work?

The personalization of jobs certainly hasn't kept pace with our experience as consumers. We expect to have our content curated, based on our viewing habits on Netflix. Amazon customizes our shopfront. Our social feeds highlight the people we're most interested in following. And yet, our work experience remains strangely lodged in the past.

The *future* of work is personalized, meaning for the first time we'll have the opportunity to focus not just on what we're good at but on what we're passionate about too.

Thanks to the internet, you can now easily connect with someone on the other side of the world who shares your interests, however niche.

As barriers to sharing our knowledge and insights with the world have reduced, it's also now far easier to engage someone willing to pay for them. As writer and *Future Work/Life* podcast guest, Dror Poleg, said:[6]

---

[6] www.drorpoleg.com/winner-takes-most/

The internet enables each of us to earn more than ever before by matching us with the exact people — fans, customers, employers — who value our unique combination of skills and characteristics. It enables each of us to become a superstar. The internet matching machine is fuelled by content. The more of it you produce, the more likely you are to reach the people who'd value what you have to offer. Writing a tweet or uploading a video costs nothing. It might be embarrassing or a waste of time, but that's about it.

You might think this is an idealistic way to think about work. 'Not everyone has unique skills and the get-up-and-go to monetize them', you might say. Well, this is where the Work/Life Flywheel comes in. By focusing on the things that bring us energy, developing a mindset of creativity and experimentation, and taking advantage of an expanding network, you can go from uninspired to unrelenting in your pursuit of your objectives.

It's all about reframing what success looks like and leveraging technology to make it happen.

THE CREATOR ECONOMY

In 2009, Kevin Kelly, the founding editor of *Wired* magazine, wrote that creators only needed to earn '1000 True Fans' – at $100 per fan per year – to make a living.

The 1,000 fans model illustrated the internet's opportunities for creators to monetize their knowledge and creativity.

To be a successful creator, you don't need millions. You don't need millions of dollars or millions of customers, millions of clients or millions of fans. To make a living as a craftsperson, photographer, musician, designer, author, animator, app maker, entrepreneur, or inventor, you need only thousands of true fans.[7]

---

[7] https://kk.org/thetechnium/1000-true-fans/

The passion economy is the next iteration of this idea.

A phrase coined by venture capitalist Li Jin, the passion economy offers creators the chance to develop an even deeper connection with their fans, who are, by extension, also their customers. Instead of charging 1,000 fans £100, why not charge 100 fans £1,000.

By the way, this isn't an empty piece of advice to just 'follow your passion'. There's no point following your passion if no one is prepared to pay you for the pleasure (more on that in Chapter 6). Rather, that the digital world has created the scale which allows us to reimagine how we can combine our expertise with something we care about. Most of us have something about which we're passionate or knowledgeable – and in many cases, both. The passion economy presents an opportunity to share this with others and, crucially, *get paid for it*.

It's less a case of 'do what you love' and more 'love what you do'.

Whenever people talk about work in these terms, it's obligatory to caveat it with an acknowledgement that not everyone has this luxury. I get it. Some people don't have the same advantages growing up, and it's impossible for every individual to perfectly craft their work/lives and do a job they're passionate about.

Here's a note of optimism, though.

As the cost to access technology reduces and the internet continues to provide an unlimited reservoir of knowledge, learning resources and, crucially, audience, new opportunities will emerge. Creating online gets easier every day, which is how we've seen the creator economy launch people from all sorts of backgrounds to success and stardom. That's not to say that a creator's lifestyle is easy. Creating unique content and sharing valuable ideas is difficult, which is why your starting point has to be a willingness to be different. To carve your own niche.

But since the most effective niches are those that combine your expertise, experience, and passions, these opportunities depend on you building a career by *being yourself*. That's got to be a good thing, right?

One last thing.

There are plenty of people who will maintain that it's unrealistic to love what you do and that work and life should remain separate. If that's you, no hard feelings but stop reading now and pass this book on to someone else. We'll look into why we need to reject the idea of work/life balance in a couple of chapters' time, but before we do, let's address the elephant in the room: 'All this sounds great, Ollie, but what if it doesn't work out?'

SUMMARY

- Life is a series of 'lifequakes' that shift how we see our place in the world.
- While 'lifequakes' are out of our control, transitions are something we choose.
- The secret to successful transitions is taking consistent, small steps and building sustainable systems.
- Changing our careers requires letting go of our status and evolving our identity.
- The future of work is personalized, and the internet enables us to connect with new opportunities and people, at scale.
- To become a creator, you need to embrace being different, focusing on where your passion and expertise overlap.

3

...Without fear

After several happy years working as a finance journalist with stints in São Paulo and Buenos Aires, Laura Price landed in Dublin, excited to start a new role closer to home in the UK.

Although she'd loved her time in South America, the job's demands had taken their toll. She was burnt out. Laura barely had time to settle into her new life before receiving some shocking news. Her Irish doctor confirmed her worst fears about a lump she'd discovered in her breast before leaving Argentina.

She was diagnosed with cancer in June 2012.

Moving immediately back to her family home, Laura put her career on hold to concentrate on treatment. Fortunately, she was in recovery a year later, but understandably, her experience permanently changed her outlook. When you encounter the fragility of life so profoundly, your priorities change. Scaling the corporate ladder doing a job she enjoyed but was never passionate about was no longer appealing. While the downsides of losing certain freedoms that come with a healthy paycheque were obvious, Laura's mindset had changed.

She had a burning desire to be creative and write about something she loved.

> I could save up X amount for this thing I really wanted to do, or I could take the leap of faith and do the project that's not going to earn me any money but will give me the satisfaction.

> I know that balance very well now. I think I even knew it in
> my early twenties, but I was too afraid at that point because
> I perhaps had to learn what the consequences could be and
> how short life was.

She'd always been fascinated by the magazine industry, so she quit her job and enrolled in a magazine journalism course.

Setting aside the financial considerations and any insecurities about starting her career again from scratch, she resolved to just follow her curiosity. As the next stage of Laura's career evolved, she was soon able to combine another of her passions – food – with her language skills, taking her to all corners of the globe to write about the world's best restaurants. Drawing on her cancer diagnosis and recovery, she also undertook the challenge of writing a novel – *Single Bald Female*, published in 2022 – allowing her to creatively inspire others with a fictional story sparked by her own experience of breast cancer.

While the life of a freelance writer isn't always easy – not least during the unpredictability of the COVID-19 pandemic – any financial uncertainty is far outweighed by the sense of fulfilment Laura gains from a work/life characterized by creativity, experimentation and constant learning.

> It's the personal satisfaction of doing something that no one
> has *asked me to do*. That came completely from my brain.
> Something I did because *I* wanted to do it.

THE REASONS HOLDING YOU BACK

For some, like Laura, life-changing events permanently and fundamentally change their perspective, but, hopefully, the reasons you're considering a work/life transition are less dramatic. Whether you're thinking about changing jobs, starting a new business, or just setting time aside for that hobby you'd abandoned, now is the time to act.

There are more opportunities to make a change than ever before, and more people are thinking about *how* to do it.

The future you're envisaging will undoubtedly be different from that of your partner, friends and colleagues. At this point, it may still feel more like a dream than a reality as you wistfully contemplate replacing a sense of mundanity with doing something you love. You may have dipped your toe in the water by starting a side project or moonlighting outside (or shh, during!) working hours. If you're particularly bold, you may even have taken the plunge and quit your job.

However, the chances are, although you've already decided you've worked one day too many securing someone else's future, you haven't yet mustered up the courage to act.

You're not alone. The reality is that, although many people want to make big changes, far fewer follow through.

Why?

Invariably, it comes down to fear of failure, which isn't a surprise when discussions about pivoting your career tend to focus on the risks – some real and some perceived.

Suppose you're like me and have a mortgage and young children. You may be wondering how the financials of your new career direction stack up against the security of your employment contract and steady income. If it doesn't work, how will you pay the bills?

And how about the fact you've never done it before? If you've only ever worked for someone else, how will you know where to start when it comes to all the tasks unrelated to your skillset. If you're a marketer, what do you know about running payroll? Running a digital marketing campaign may seem like a mystery if you work in finance, and if you're a designer, where do you start when it comes to trying to win new clients?

The final reason that most frequently comes up in my research is reputational risk.

What if it doesn't work out, and will I look like an idiot? What will people think of me if I don't get it right? How will I look at myself in the mirror if I quit my successful job and try something that fails?

HOW TO AVOID REGRET

Ok, so I get all that.

There are always reasons not to do something. The thing is, there's an even bigger reason to take the leap, but to understand why, we have to cast our minds into the future and look at our choice through the lens of regret. Quite simply, you're more likely to regret *inaction* than *action*.

In Daniel Pink's research for his book, *The Power of Regret*, he ran a global survey asking people to share their greatest regret. Among the nearly 20,000 people who contributed, the overwhelming wish when looking back was that they'd adopted more of a *bias for action*. And the greater the time that passes, the more profound the sense of regret.

As Dan explained to me on the *Future Work/Life* podcast, people often rue their failure to act boldly in their work and personal lives.

As one of four key types of regret we experience – the others being foundational, moral and maintaining connections – *boldness* regrets, in particular, grow stronger over time. Looking back in 20 years, our negative feelings towards our lack of action into starting something new will only get stronger.

> We have a very good sense of what future-you is going to regret. Future-you is going to regret not building a stable foundation for your life. Future-you is going to regret **not taking an appropriate risk**. Future-you is going to regret not doing the right thing and future-you is going to regret not building connections to people you love. And that's it.

It turns out that failing to be bold is far riskier in the long run than failing in a new venture.

As a thought exercise, imagine yourself 20 years in the future, looking back on the decisions you make now. How would you feel if you didn't follow through when you're confident in your abilities, knowledge, and capacity to learn? Back in the present, this 'what if?' question elicits the same insights every time: most people wish they'd spoken up more, made the jump into going it alone, and set up the business they've always dreamed of.

There's also value and learning to be had in confronting regrets about decisions we've already made. Understanding our emotions teaches us lessons about ourselves and how to make better decisions in the future.

REFRAMING OUR EMOTIONS

Regret is an emotion, just like happiness or sadness. The trick to using emotions positively is *first* to reframe how we perceive the reasons for experiencing them and, even more significantly, how we talk to ourselves about them.

Dr Kristin Neff, a psychology professor at the University of Texas, is a leading expert on why our 'inner voice' can determine how emotions manifest and affect every aspect of our lives.[8] Her work shows that people who demonstrate more 'self-compassion' are happier, more satisfied with life, better motivated, and physically healthier. They also maintain stronger relationships, are less anxious, less prone to depression and more resilient.

So how do we foster more self-compassion?

- Be kind to yourself and non-judgemental about the decisions you make.
- Recognize that making mistakes is 'human', and everyone experiences the same feeling at different points in their lives.
- Face up to failure and pain with equanimity – a calm, mindful acceptance that the world and your life is how it is, flaws and all.

When I spoke to Damian Hughes, organizational psychologist and co-host of the chart-topping *High Performance* podcast, he explained how he'd learned the importance of self-compassion the hard way.

A few years before, he'd found himself in hospital, burned out and seriously ill because of the pace of his work and his failure to prioritize

---

[8] Dr Kristin Neff, *Self Compassion: The Proven Power of Being Kind to Yourself*, Yellow Kite, 2011.

self-care. As many of us fall prey to, Damian was brutal in how he spoke to himself about the relentless need to keep pushing when he should have been taking a break and slowing down. It was only after reflecting on how he'd view it if someone spoke to his son the way he talked to himself that he could gain perspective and break the damaging habits.

Now, kindness to himself is one of his 'non-negotiables' – something on which he won't compromise.

The *second* stage of facing up to and learning from your emotions is disclosure. Acknowledging and labelling your feelings helps unburden you from the worries, and can alleviate anxiety and lower the risk of depression. As Dan Pink says:

> You take this blobby, negative abstraction, which is looming and amorphous, and you convert it into language either by writing or talking about it. You make it go from abstract to concrete, and go from menacing to far less fearsome. That begins the sense-making process.

While many fear that people will think less of us when we reveal our feelings, the opposite is true. Other people's opinions of us improve when we can recognize and act upon our anxieties, past mistakes and regrets.

The *final* stage is to look forward and extract a lesson from your feelings that you can act upon. Damian Hughes touched on one trick for achieving this – thinking about how we'd advise a family member or friend grants us an objective view, free of internal bias. So, if you're deliberating over a difficult choice, picture what you'd tell your best friend if they came to you with the same dilemma.

- Not sure whether to quit your job and follow your passion for gardening? Knowing everything you know, how would you advise your friend?
- Considering moving to Ibiza with the family but worried how that might affect your opportunities to work with clients in person? How would you feel if someone you're close to shared that they were thinking about making the move? Envious? Relieved you don't have to do the same?

The answers are in there somewhere, you may just need to look at the question from a different viewpoint.

TALKING TO YOURSELF

If there's no one you can picture sharing the advice with, how about a spot of 'illeism' – talking to yourself in the third person?

Talking about yourself to yourself requires mentally stepping back and gaining perspective on an issue. The benefits are not just that it can help you calm down. It helps reframe problems that seem insurmountable and gives you more confidence. You can also combine this with 'temporal distancing' – projecting your thoughts to the future – to separate yourself from all-consuming short-term worries. Again, the distance can help both dampen anxiety and improve performance. For example, if we regret making a bold choice about our careers ten years ago, we can use that to inform our decision-making today.

Let's consider that moving to Ibiza question that I posed before:

'Ollie if you decide to up sticks to Ibiza, you'll be creating unnecessary disruption in your kids' lives'

'I know that, Ollie, but imagine how amazing it will be for them to learn Spanish and be able to go straight to the beach after school every day.'

'Yes, but what are you going to do when a new client asks you to come to the office to see them the next day?'

'I'd probably say what century are you living in, and, anyway, my aim is to have a business that can be run from anywhere in the world, so this is the perfect way to test it. And besides, if it doesn't work out, we'll come home having experienced something new as a family.'

Dammit, maybe I should have made that move to Ibiza after all.

LIVING IN THE FUTURE

Adopting the mental model of living in the future can help improve your short- and long-term decision-making.

I spent two years examining how to learn from the successes and failures in my past to plan the next stage of my career. In research for this book, I interviewed and surveyed thousands of others wrangling with the same anxieties and worries. I agree with Dan Pink that it's far more likely that we'll experience regret when we fail to be bold, but it can take time to build the confidence to follow your own path and pursue a work/life that marries your passion with your expertise.

However, by approaching the process with the right mindset, and combining creativity and experimentation with the support of your community – by building your Work/Life Flywheel – you will be successful.

Soon, we'll explore how you can start designing yours, but before then, I'll explain what this flywheel thing is all about and why we should be using this as a mental model rather than that tired and damaging idea of *balance*.

SUMMARY

- Going it alone isn't easy, but financial uncertainty is often outweighed by the fulfilment you get from a work/life characterized by creativity, experimentation and constant learning.
- With more opportunities than ever before, to make a change, now is the perfect time to take action.
- Most people don't do it because of a fear of failure, but you're more likely to regret inaction than action.
- Self-compassion helps you become happier, healthier, better motivated and more satisfied with life.
- Facing up to your emotions and revealing them to others alleviates anxiety and lowers the risk of depression.
- Imagining you're talking to a friend or talking to yourself gives you a detached, objective view of your decision.
- Using the mental model of living in the future improves your short- and long-term decision making.

4

Forget balance, you need a flywheel

I've always found language fascinating.

Mastering foreign languages grants you very particular privileges, for example. Namely, engaging with a whole group of people with whom you would, otherwise, only be able to communicate via gesticulation. Yes, increasingly, English is becoming the second language of many of the world's population, but the ability to share ideas, thoughts, or even just ask for directions in someone else's native tongue remains a satisfying feeling.

I'm equally interested in the written language. Particularly in those who appear to effortlessly craft sentences that perfectly articulate an opinion or know exactly which words to use when explaining something complex to make it accessible and easily understood.

None of which is to say that words matter more than actions – we all know that phrase, after all. Only to highlight that semantics – the meaning of those words – are important and can influence how we feel about a person or subject.

So, with that in mind, f**k work/life balance.

That's a bit strong, you might say. What's wrong with aspiring for balance? Surely you're not advocating that work take priority over your personal life? Or, for that matter, arguing that work doesn't matter at all?

Of course not.

I'm simply suggesting that balance is the wrong metaphor. To perfectly balance work and life is impossible. For a start, how do you even measure it? Maybe when you're feeling unquestionably happy and fulfilled in both? Fair enough, but let's be honest, those moments can feel fleeting for many of us. Plus, it can be challenging to pinpoint precisely what changes from one day to the next, as your perception of achieving 'balance' shifts.

IF NOT BALANCE, THEN WHAT?

For the past 30 years, Stew Friedman's Work/Life Integration Project at Wharton School of Business has studied how people's work and private lives intersect. Friedman's work has consistently shown that as people pursue this unachievable notion of balance, they're often left overwhelmed and unfulfilled.

In *Parents Who Lead*, he and Alyssa Westring wrote about how parents could take a more realistic approach to designing their work/ lives, taking into account four common areas of life – work, home/ family, community, self.

When Alyssa and I explored these ideas together on the podcast, she explained how, through their research and work with parents and business leaders, they've found that recognizing the connection between the four areas is critical to success and wellbeing. Embracing how they integrate with one another can empower you to feel greater purpose and harmony across all parts of your life.

As Stew Friedman wrote in *Leading the Life You Want:*[9]

> You can't have it all – complete success in all the corners of
> your life, all at the same time. No one can. But even though
> it can seem impossible to bring these four domains into
> greater alignment, it doesn't have to be impossible. Conflict
> and stress aren't inevitable. Harmony is possible.

---

[9] Stewart D. Friedman, *Leading the Life You Want: Skills for Integrating Work and Life*, Harvard Business Review Press, 2014.

Integration. Alignment. Harmony.

Each a far better metaphor for the relationship between every aspect of our lives than *balance*, but still not right. While accepting ebbs and flows is a healthy and necessary step, improving the likelihood of a harmonious life is still in your hands. You're not looking for momentary satisfaction but to constantly progress. To feel a sense of momentum building from the decisions you make and the actions you take.

Which is why, for a solution, I turned to a resource in which I've found so many answers over the years: business books. Specifically, management frameworks. Yes, I know what you're thinking. And it's true, I love spreadsheets too!

MANAGEMENT FRAMEWORKS

Why do some ideas break into mainstream consciousness?

In some cases, a phrase captures the zeitgeist so profoundly that we forget about the individual who coined it. Take FOMO – fear of missing out – for example. An acronym that perfectly encapsulates the emotions of a generation brought up on social media. A phrase used so ubiquitously that you might imagine it had emerged organically rather than from a guy whose job is to look for patterns in behaviour to help shape investment strategies. Namely, venture capitalist Patrick McGinnis.

Similarly, if you've read any book about entrepreneurship since 2011, it likely borrowed the language of Eric Ries' *The Lean Start-Up*. The idea of a 'minimum-viable-product' is now universally understood as shorthand for something just good enough to test.

These phrases are adopted at scale because they succinctly capture an idea, mood, or feeling. Add a metaphor to the equation, and they become even more appealing, bringing to life otherwise abstract concepts.

Legendary management author and researcher Jim Collins has a particular knack for this. Even if you've not read his 1994 book, *Built to Last*, an all-time business bestseller, you'll probably have heard of its stand-out idea. Why talk about big goals, Collins thought, when Big Hairy Audacious Goals (BHAG) stick in the mind, and presumably the throat, so much better?

THE FLYWHEEL EFFECT

It's to Jim Collins that we all owe a word of thanks for popularizing the flywheel effect.

Flywheel is not as colourful a term as BHAG. Nor is it as immediately impactful a name as the Hedgehog Concept, another of Collins' famous ideas. After all, who isn't intrigued by how a small, spiky creature prone to long periods of hibernation and often on the wrong end of a speeding vehicle, relates to business. However, the beauty of the flywheel is that with only a little explanation and framing, it becomes a lens through which you view every successful company and product.

Trust me, I do it all the time, and by the time you've read this book, you'll start to do the same.

In Collins' words:[10]

> No matter how dramatic the end result, good-to-great transformations never happen in one fell swoop. In building a great company or social sector enterprise, there is no single defining action, no grand program, no one killer innovation, no solitary lucky break, no miracle moment. Rather, the process resembles relentlessly pushing a giant, heavy flywheel, turn upon turn, building momentum until a point of breakthrough, and beyond.

Jim Collins successfully translated that sensation that so many founders and entrepreneurs experience in the early days, when it feels like you're pushing a bloody great wheel up a hill with very little assistance. You just about manage to get the thing moving but not without a serious amount of strain and a large dollop of doubt about whether it's worth it. But you keep on pushing and by the second turn, it becomes a little easier. By the tenth rotation, there's a sense that the wheel's weight, rather than impeding its progress, may actually be helping you move it.

---

[10] Jim Collins, *Good to Great: Why Some Companies Make the Leap... and Others Don't*, Random House Business, 2001.

If you stopped pushing here, the wheel would quickly grind to a halt, but by keeping the momentum up, the speed gradually increases and, before you know it, the wheel appears to be moving entirely of its own volition.

In a great business, no single part of this flywheel is more important than any other – they're interdependent. While the composition of each flywheel differs depending on the industry, customer need, and the expertise of the people activating the plan, the result is a virtuous circle of value creation.

AMAZON'S VIRTUOUS CIRCLE

Robert Burgelman was Jim Collins' professor at the Stanford School of Business in 1982. One of his perceptive but straightforward observations influenced Collins' work and one of the business world's modern success stories.

> 'The greatest danger in business and life,' he explained, 'lies not in outright failure but in achieving success without understanding why you were successful in the first place.'[11]

In 2001, Amazon's destiny as one of the world's most successful and innovative companies was by no means guaranteed. For years, Amazon. com, as it was then known, had been written off by the traditional business press as a company built on sand. Take the front cover of financial magazine *Barron*, which in 1999 carried the headline, 'Amazon. bomb'. They wrote:

> The idea that Amazon CEO Jeff Bezos has pioneered a new business paradigm is silly. He's just another middleman, and the stock market is beginning to catch on to that fact.

Oops.

---

[11] Jim Collins, *Turning the Flywheel: A Monograph to Accompany Good to Great*, Harper Business, 2019.

At that point, though, the doomsayers looked like they might be right as the fallout of the dot-com bust was felt all around them.

With this backdrop, in 2001 Jim Collins sat down with Jeff Bezos and a group of Amazon executives to share the insights he'd recently published in his book, *Good to Great*. The flywheel idea immediately resonated with Bezos, who instinctively recognized the significance of the effect of 'strategic compounding' that was the central idea of the framework.

Much as the compounding effect of interest ultimately leads to wealth creation, a good decision built upon a good decision, repeated many times over, will propel a business to greatness.

Bezos and his team set about designing their own flywheel, built on their obsession with creating customer value.

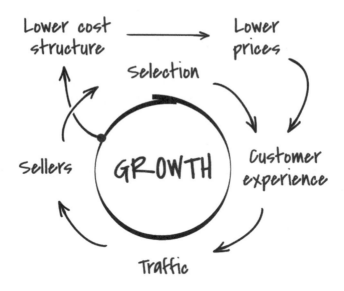

In the early days of online shopping, limited availability and cataloguing of products and a generally clunky check-out process added up to a poor user experience. Amazon understood that increasing the number of shoppers required removing this friction.

As traffic increased to the site, it created an opportunity for Amazon to invite third parties to sell their products through the platform, creating an open marketplace rather than a traditional retailer model. As volumes went up, they established a fulfilment service for vendors, making it easier to match supply with demand. More sellers led to a broader selection of products, making it even easier for customers to find what they were looking for whenever they needed it.

All of which contributed to a constantly improving customer experience, completing the virtuous circle.

As with any business model flywheel, the model wasn't static. It was constantly in motion, evolving and expanding. As the retail business's growth led to lower cost structures, they could lower their prices, further enhancing customer experience and making the flywheel spin even faster.

SPINNING OFF INTO OTHER PRODUCTS AND SERVICES

The process also created unintended and unexpected opportunities, leading to the creation of Amazon Web Services (AWS).

The exponential growth of their retail business meant the company was consistently and rapidly scaling up its technical infrastructure. In practical terms, this required building huge server farms, in which millions of computers combined to create what we now call 'cloud storage'. Initially, the cloud storage enabled the Amazon website to cope with vast amounts of traffic without interruption, but as the technical architecture improved, Bezos spotted another opportunity.

Since cloud storage requires significant capital investment and highly-skilled engineers to maintain, how about once again inviting other vendors to the party?

AWS soon emerged as the gold standard for cloud computing, and as its ecosystem quickly developed, it achieved ever-improving economies of scale, higher-quality applications and better customer support.

All of which led to, you guessed it, enhanced customer experience and more demand from businesses looking for a cloud solution. The flywheel keeps on turning.

Amazon leveraged the idea to create not just one but multiple successful products, but the flywheel isn't only supposed to be a retrospective analysis of a successful business. Nor is it a definitive playbook from which we can design the perfect product or service. Instead, it's a metaphor that illustrates how we combine individual components to become greater than the sum of their parts.

YOUR WORK/LIFE FLYWHEEL

So let's break down how we'll approach designing each part of your Work/Life Flywheel to help you reimagine your work/life.

Because as James Clear said in his bestselling book, *Atomic Habits:*[12]

> You do not rise to the level of your goals. You fall to the level of your systems.

The Work/Life Flywheel *is* the system.

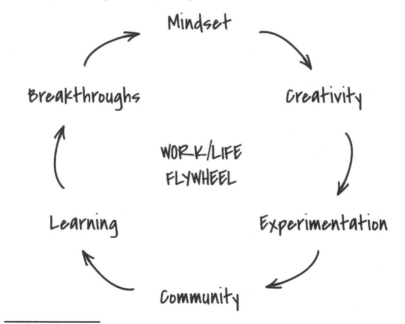

---

[12] James Clear, *Atomic Habits: An Easy and Proven Way to Build Good Habits and Break Bad Ones*, Random House Business, 2018.

While the individual components of every business flywheel are different, what's common to all of them is that no single part is any more important than any other.

The only way the flywheel can start turning is for everything to work together in harmony, with each component feeding into the next until momentum builds between them and we create the virtuous circle. Although we all have unique characteristics, goals, and talents, there are six building blocks common to every successful approach.

1. Mindset
2. Creativity
3. Experimentation
4. Community
5. Learning
6. Breakthroughs

So, where do we begin?

Before starting any mission, you'd better be sure you want to do it. Given you've bought this book and read it this far, I assume that you understand this and are ready to work hard to design a new, improved work/life. And that's the first step – developing a progressive but pragmatic MINDSET that focuses on being clear about your values and objectives.

Building on your intrinsic motivations and goals, we'll then focus on how they feed into adopting CREATIVITY as a core value. Creativity will be the differentiator in the future of work, so we'll explore how to develop a habit of thinking differently and telling stories that matter to people.

Creativity demands that we accept that not everything we try will work out as planned, which is the next crucial part of the model. Developing an attitude of constant EXPERIMENTATION in our work/lives will unlock new levels of insight and help us establish our expert niche while exposing us to new and exciting opportunities and connections.

Legendary innovators need the support of others, which is why we'll examine the importance of your COMMUNITY. With the right combination of strong and weak ties, and diverse knowledge and opinions, you'll discover your speed of learning accelerates.

We need to adopt a new approach to lifelong LEARNING that takes account of longer life expectancy and our work/lives taking multiple paths as our careers evolve. We'll therefore dip into why you need to take a long-term view and to constantly follow your curiosity.

As you construct your Flywheel, I'll show you why taking a step back to reflect and recognize your progress is the final piece in the puzzle. While making big changes in your career can be tough, it shouldn't all be hard work. To realize the benefits of everything you're doing, you need time to rest and recover, which is when you achieve BREAKTHROUGHS that give you the intrinsic rewards and motivational boosts that feed your positive MINDSET.

And so the circle is complete, and the wheel spins again. And again. And again.

Excited? Me too. Let's stop talking about the theory and crack on.

──────────── SUMMARY ────────────

- Perfectly balancing work and life is impossible.
- Rather than looking for momentary harmony, you need a model that enables constant progress.
- The flywheel effect occurs when all parts of a business model are interdependent and complementary, creating a virtuous circle.
- Amazon built multiple businesses by designing flywheels built on an obsession with creating customer value.
- An effective flywheel is never static – it's constantly in motion, evolving and expanding.
- What's common to every flywheel is that no single part is more important than any other – they have to work together in harmony.
- The Work/Life Flywheel is built using six interconnected elements – Mindset, Creativity, Experimentation, Community, Learning and Breakthroughs.

PART 2

THE WORK/LIFE FLYWHEEL

Mindset

Mindset

Breakthroughs

Creativity

WORK/LIFE
FLYWHEEL

Learning

Experimentation

Community

5

Keeping an open mind

Compare these two well-known phrases:

Some people have all the luck.

You make your own luck in life.

Two sentences. Two completely different outlooks on life.

The first is a begrudging acceptance that life happens to us. The second acknowledges that we have agency over our choices and life's outcomes.

So, which one is it? Are some people really luckier than others?

Christian Busch is so fascinated by these questions that he has spent years thinking about them and wrote a book about the subject. He first distinguishes between what we think of as 'blind luck' – the stuff that happens to us – and serendipity, or 'smart luck'. For example, some degree of randomness is inevitable in life, and we're never in complete control of what happens – take the involuntary lifequakes we discussed in Chapter 1 as an example. However, as Christian's work shows, it *is* possible to cultivate more serendipity.

How? By keeping an open mind and being led by curiosity.

Take the 'five-pound note' experiment conducted by British psychology professor Richard Wiseman.[13] Designed to test self-perception, researchers took people who identified as either 'extremely lucky' or 'extremely unlucky'. They asked them to walk down a street to a coffee shop, buy a coffee and sit down. Hidden cameras tracked their moves, including when they stepped over a five-pound note that had been placed at the coffee shop entrance. They'd also rearranged the tables in the café, placing a successful businessman in the seat next to the counter.

Guess what happened?

The 'lucky' people, including Marvellous Martin, spotted the note, picked it up, then went inside and sat next to the businessman after ordering their coffee. They started a conversation and became friends.

What about Bothersome Brenda, our 'unlucky' participant (the names are real, by the way, although I've added the adjectives for a bit of colour)?

Not only did she miss the cash, but she also stayed silent despite sitting in the spot next to the businessman. Needless to say, after Wiseman's team asked Bothersome Brenda how her day had gone, she wasn't brimming with optimism. In contrast to Marvellous Martin, who was buzzing about what a great day he'd had.

Two people. Precisely the same conditions and opportunities. Two entirely different outcomes.

As Christian summarized:

Openness to the unexpected is key to being lucky – and to experience serendipity.[14]

THE HOOK

So, if serendipity is part of an intentional outlook on life, how can you get better at making your own luck?

---

[13] Richard Wiseman, *The Luck Factor: The Scientific Study of the Lucky Mind*, Arrow, 2004.

[14] Dr Christian Busch, *The Serendipity Mindset: The Art and Science of Creating Good Luck*, Penguin Life, 2020.

Let's start with how you greet people. What's your go-to question when you meet someone new at a party? If it's 'what do you do?', I've got some news for you – life is about to get a lot more interesting!

Whether it's 'what do you do?', 'how was your weekend?' or 'are you going anywhere nice', writer David Sedaris rails against the mundanity of these sorts of questions. He prefers openers like: 'when was the last time you touched a monkey', which, in his case, elicited the reply, 'oh, can you smell it on me?'[15]

A step too far for many perhaps, but the point here is that obvious, tired questions don't reveal much about the person you're speaking to and significantly reduce your chance of finding common ground. So, why not try something different, such as, 'what do you enjoy doing?' or 'what are you most excited about over the next three months?'

If you're on the receiving end of the 'what do you do?' question, on the other hand, try a 'hook strategy'.

Using 'serendipity hooks' gives people the chance to learn more about you and allows them the possibility to make connections between *your* interests and experiences and *theirs*. Since they asked, you may as well share what you do for work, but also go a step further and volunteer *more* information to give your new acquaintance a sense of who you really are. Christian Busch shares a great example of how you might do this in his book, *Connect the Dots: The Art and Science of Creating Good Luck*:[16]

> I love connecting people, have been active in the education sector, and recently started thinking about philosophy, but what I really enjoy is playing the piano.

The 'hook strategy' allows people to discover what they find interesting about you and vice versa. All it takes is to be open-minded about trying something different and stimulating more opportunities to make connections.

---

[15] David Sedaris, *A Carnival of Snackery: Diaries 2003–2020*, Little, Brown, 2021.

[16] Dr Christian Busch, *Connect the Dots: The Art and Science of Creating Good Luck*, Penguin Life, 2022.

BROADENING YOUR HORIZONS

Rethinking your approach to greetings is just one example of why cultivating serendipity relies on a willingness to do things differently.

Now I work from home most of the time, life can feel repetitive. I tend to slip into the same routines every day, which has meant feeling like I'm stuck in a rut at different times. One way I've tackled this is to force myself out of my comfort zone. In no way has this been as evident as in my newfound love of building new relationships. After working in the same industry for over ten years, I had to broaden my horizons. I made a conscious decision to connect with new people every week, which was a radical change in my mindset.

As well as overcoming my natural reluctance to network, I developed a mindset that embraced any new opportunity that arose.

A simple shift in attitude and behaviour has led to new collaborations, paid gigs and friendships that have opened my eyes to subjects I never even knew existed. They sparked new levels of creativity and, after ongoing experimentation, gave me new knowledge and countless breakthroughs that ultimately contributed to me writing this book. Crucially, these new experiences allowed me to experiment with what I wanted to do next in my career.

Zen Buddhism refers to this mindset as Shoshin – 'beginner's mind' – an openness, enthusiasm and a lack of preconceptions about a subject, however long you've studied it.

As Buddhist monk Shunryū Suzuki put it:

> In the beginner's mind there are many possibilities but in the expert's there are few.

To maximize the value of this book, I'm going to ask you to approach your work/life with Shoshin. Think about new ways of doing things that have become routine and consider existing and new relationships with a sense of possibility. Keep your eyes open for the unexpected. Make connections between parts of your life that complement one another and create a virtuous circle.

If you're a practical person, then great, there are habits you can develop in your working day which will help you take a new perspective.

For example, many of us sit in weekly meetings with our team and reflect on the highlight of the previous week. I certainly used to do this and found it a great way of recognizing people's contributions and progress. But how about you also ask everyone to share something unexpected that happened? As well as reminding everyone that not everything goes exactly to plan in work or life, we'd learn something entirely different about everyone's role and their experience throughout the week. What's more, encouraging people to think about unpredictability positively demonstrates the value of the unanticipated, even if things don't always work out.

These mindset shifts are necessary to thrive in a VUCA world – volatile, uncertain, complex and ambiguous.

An open mind also extends to the potential of people, including ourselves. Christian shared a brilliant quote with me, which resonated when I thought about how it relates to our experiences of overcoming difficult circumstances:

If you want a happy ending, don't end the story too early.

It's easy to write ourselves and others off after making mistakes or experiencing 'failures', yet by reframing these events as precursors to the next stage of our lives, we can turn them into lessons that define our future.

KEEPING YOUR EYES OPEN

Inspiration can arrive at any time, anywhere. For Emma Freivogel, it just happened to be while on stage.

For 17 years, she'd worked with 'the underdogs of society'. People for whom working and contributing as a member of society was far from guaranteed and who live with labels like 'gang members, black, homeless, gay'. She recognized the privileged position she was in as she matched them with whichever jobs were left over. The roles that she told me, 'British people mostly don't want to do'.

Yet, while these offered a great start for some, so many others should and could have far greater opportunities open to them.

The debate at the event at which she was speaking was aimed at 'innovative and forward-leaning people' and focused on tackling discrimination in the labour market. Despite there being 35,000 recruitment agencies registered as trading in the UK, they were largely inaccessible to anyone from an 'unconventional background'.

One of her fellow panellists was living proof of the challenges this presented, and yet, at the same time, Rachel offered an inspiring reason for optimism.

Rachel had most recently left prison 18 months before that afternoon sitting on the stage with Emma. She'd experienced a tumultuous life. Her childhood was characterized by abuse and neglect. She had been in a spiral that resulted in 43 convictions, and yo-yo'd in and out of institutions. Not an unusual story for the people Emma worked with.

However, Rachel bravely refused to continue on this journey and took bold actions to change her life and those of other inmates.

She negotiated the governor's approval to set up an enterprise in prison, which was not an easy feat for anyone, even an organization like Emma's. Rachel was determined to create a functioning operation to help participants learn skills they could use when they re-entered the community. In her case, she'd always wanted to work in the food industry, and after securing a deal to cater an event, one of the guests happened to be the owner of a well-known restaurant chain in London. When he tried Rachel's carrot cake, he told her it was the best he'd ever eaten and offered her a job on the spot.

A year and a half later, Rachel left prison, took the job and worked her way up from kitchen assistant to head chef in training. She hasn't reoffended and has rebuilt her life.

While listening to Rachel tell her story, Emma couldn't help but think if all it takes is one piece of carrot cake, what else might be possible. Like for the tens of thousands of other offenders in the UK. Or the 14 million people with disabilities denied the opportunity to contribute because people aren't open-minded enough to look past stereotypes.

One month before the COVID-19 lockdowns came into force, Emma set up her recruitment business for the 'radically different'. She played her part not just in creating new possibilities for those on the wrong end of disadvantages, but in opening the minds of business leaders to benefit from the advantages of a more diverse workforce.

As Emma explained to me:

> The people we represent as a collective have three things in abundance that I would say their counterparts in the mainstream don't: resilience, self-determination and sheer grit. People who have those three things are those who push forward and get through. They really appreciate the opportunities they've got because they haven't always had them.

It's difficult to set up a business at any time and in any sector, but creating a not-for-profit in the middle of a global pandemic presented significant obstacles. From talking with Emma, though, you quickly recognize her steely determination to support others to overcome their disadvantages and maximize their potential. Every message she receives from candidates thanking her for 'treating me like a human', and notes from employers who recognize their new employees' contributions, gives her fresh encouragement that things are changing.

> When you see people you've helped give back, come back and give to the community. That's how I keep going. But I need to sleep more. And I need a holiday!

Whether you're inspired to make a real difference to the lives of others, like Emma, or take this opportunity to change your own, now's the time.

If you're still wondering where to start, the answer lies in this question: what really matters to you?

SUMMARY

- You're never in complete control of your life, but you can cultivate more serendipity by keeping an open mind and following your curiosity.
- Using a hook strategy allows you and others to connect your interests and theirs.
- Embracing new opportunities sparks new levels of creativity, learning and breakthroughs.
- Preparing for and recognizing the value of the unexpected helps you get comfortable when things don't always go to plan.
- Reframing mistakes and 'failures' as learning opportunities enables you to realize the benefits of open-mindedness about yourself and others.
- With the right mindset, the greater the obstacle you experience, the stronger and more determined you become.

6

Your north star

When you've been the best in the world in your field and pioneered its transition to a professional sport, starting your career afresh isn't straightforward.

Brought up in apartheid South Africa, Shaun Tomson was raised with a love of the ocean despite his father, one of the country's best swimmers in his youth, having his Olympic swimming dreams ruined by a shark attack. Both of his parents had emigrated to the country during the Second World War. His Jewish father fled the Nazis, and his mother escaped her home in Malta, which remains the most heavily bombed place in any conflict throughout history. Having sailed away from the horrors of war, the sea became a hallowed place for the Tomson family.

Amid the separation and hate that characterized that period in South African history, Shaun recognized the power that surfing had to bring people together.

Along with a group of young Australians and Hawaiians, Shaun introduced a new approach to what was previously a niche activity for a limited few, based in random hotspots around the world. He and his fellow 'founders' created what became as much a lifestyle as a sport. They merged their love of competition and pursuing the limits of human capability with an ethos of sharing and supporting one another.

Fifty years later, the surfing industry generates billions of dollars a year and has influenced popular culture across the globe.

It's certainly a long way from where he started as a 14-year-old competing for waves with people twice his age. Having worked his way up through local and then international events, he became world champion, competing with the very best for more than two decades. At the end of his career, he stepped away from competition but stayed connected with surfing. Initially, he ran the surfing division for Patagonia, the clothing company, before setting up his own brand with his wife, Carla.

However, it was years later when his true path revealed itself to him and defined how he'd spend the remainder of his life.

THE CODE

In 2006, Shaun and his wife lost their 15-year-old son, Matthew, to a tragic accident. While life would never be the same, Shaun later reflected on how something he'd created several years before – The Surfers Code – could inspire him to share a message of positivity and hope with others. In the process, he produced a framework for people to find *their* purpose.

When he'd originally written The Code, he drew on his experience and love of the ocean to share metaphors that resonated with our journey through life, such as:

- I will never turn my back on the ocean.
- All surfers are joined by one ocean.
- There will always be another wave.
- I will watch out for other surfers.
- I will catch a wave every day.

After being approached while in the line-up (the queue for waves in layman's speak) on his adopted home beach in Santa Barbara, he gave a talk at a local school about how the kids could use The Code to help define how they wanted to live their lives. By asking them to start each sentence with 'I will', Shaun encouraged the children to think about committing to what they believed in.

The very first contribution he read was from a young girl who wrote:

I will always be myself.

The meaning of this simple line affected Shaun profoundly as he reflected on the importance of this idea for young people.

> I'd lost my beautiful son, fifteen years old, to a bad choice to play a dangerous game he'd heard about at school. So, now I read this first line – 'I will be myself'. I don't know whether my son played this game because of a peer pressure thing. Who knows? We'll never know, but those words spoke to me and I went down a completely different path. I started speaking at schools and getting kids to write their codes.

He has now shared The Code with hundreds of thousands of people worldwide, in schools and in businesses. Collectively, they've created millions of lines of what Shaun calls 'open-sourced code'. He shared two key insights with me from all that data:

- We're all born to be connected.
- We're born to be better.

In Shaun's words, his life has been marked by 'success, failure, happiness and terrible tragedy'. His purpose is now to encourage people to identify their values, to encourage children to take the right path and, in doing so, to keep the spirit of his son alive. Shaun has inspired me in many ways. Specifically, after we spoke, I sat down with my wife and children and had the wonderful experience of discussing what's most important to us.

So, with some grammatical correction and minor editing from me (for clarity), here's their/our Family Code. I think you'll find it's relevant whatever age you are:

- I will be kind.
- I will never show off.
- I will always be honest.
- I will look after animals.
- I will always cuddle my family.
- I will think positively about every day.
- I will be thankful for everything I have.

- I will always play and have fun; every day.
- I will eat with my family and try new food.
- I will listen to what other people have to say.
- I will share how I feel with those close to me.
- I will try new things even if it's difficult and won't be embarrassed if I don't get them right the first time.

Wise words from some helpful kids.

HOW TO LIVE BY YOUR VALUES

The Code is one way of establishing what matters to you, but how do you stick with it?

Do you ever find yourself compromising on your values? If so, how would things change if you considered them as non-negotiable standards from which you'll never deviate? As I discussed with author and organizational psychologist Damian Hughes, framing your values as non-negotiables removes ambiguity from your decision-making process.

By stipulating the standards you'll stick to without fail, you're making your priorities clear to yourself, your family and friends, and the people you work with.

In some extreme cases, like that of Stephen Hendry, one of snooker's most successful players, his non-negotiable objective to be the most dominant individual in the sport's history meant sacrificing everything else, including his family. He was unrelenting in his pursuit of what he perceived as greatness, acknowledging that he couldn't and wouldn't change who he was.

While I wouldn't make the same choices as Stephen Hendry, I can understand how such a singular and relentless focus on winning contributed to his achievements.

Commitment to anything in life requires making a choice – not just to pursue that goal, but to *ignore* the millions of other things that could take up the finite time we have available to us. Discussing this idea can be valuable in itself, as it helps you find alignment with those around you. For instance, our mutual desire for kindness and fun in our lives led to a shared understanding and sense of connection between myself and Damian Hughes.

Likewise, suppose you have a passion for caring for animals, exploring the possibilities of science, or pushing the limits of physical performance. In each case, by expressing their significance, you'll find a tribe of others that can relate. And it can often be the backing of these people that inspires and motivates you during those inevitable periods in work and life when progress seems to stall.

Kanter's Law, a theory based on Rosabeth Moss Kanter's work,[17] describes how in the middle of any period of change – whether a work project, a career transition or becoming a parent – you'll experience a sense that everything is failing. It's precisely at this point that non-negotiables, and a crystal-clear focus on the outcomes we're aiming for, can help push us through. Take the idea of a 'north star' – an overarching goal that you continually use to orient yourself in the right direction. During what Brene Brown calls the 'messy middle'[18] – when you're ready to pack it in and give up – a reminder and reassessment of your original purpose gives you fresh impetus.

In this scenario, ask yourself these questions:

- Are you still inspired by your vision for the future, and are those around you still willing to support you in achieving it?
- Can you identify progress you've already made, including tangible milestones and indicators that you're on the right track to succeed?
- Is there anything else you're doing that can help reignite your energy and reinvigorate your motivation?

During our conversation, Damian reminded me of a quote from Stephen Covey's classic book, *The 7 Habits of Highly Effective People*,[19]

---

[17] https://hbr.org/2009/08/change-is-hardest-in-the-middl
[18] Brene Brown, *Rising Strong: How the Ability to Reset Transforms the Way We Live, Love, Parent, and Lead*, Random House, 2015.
[19] Stephen R. Covey, *The 7 Habits of Highly Effective People: Powerful Lessons in Personal Change*, Simon & Schuster, 2013.

which emphasizes another reason for regularly reflecting on your vision for the future.

As Covey puts it, 'beginning with the end in mind' requires you:

> [know] where you're going so that you better understand where you are now and so that the steps you take are always in the right direction. It's incredibly easy to get caught up in an activity trap, in the busy-ness of life, to work harder and harder at climbing the ladder of success only to discover it's leaning against the wrong wall.

In other words, during those inevitably tricky times we all experience, it helps to reaffirm that our destination is worth the struggle and the many small steps to get there. You certainly don't want to look back and wonder 'what was the point of it all?' You can approach this in three distinct phases:

- The outcome – your 'north star'.
- Measurable performance targets that show you're on the right track.
- The everyday process to achieve these goals.

Consider Dina Asher-Smith, for example, who, as I write, is Britain's fastest female athlete.

Dina's mission in life is based entirely on the person she wants to be and the difference she wants to make – specifically, being a role model for young girls and proving that anyone can break the glass ceiling and achieve greatness.

Since reaching this milestone is challenging to quantify, her performance targets are specific and tangible – winning world and Olympic medals. To fulfil this ambition requires dedication and hard work, which, in her case, equates to five track sessions and three visits to the physio every week while constantly maintaining a disciplined approach to nutrition and diet. Critically, she also schedules time to take a step back, recover, and reflect on her progress, which is a vital element of her trusting the process.

There's an expression I've heard Damian use on the *High Performance* podcast – which he presents with Jake Humphrey – that neatly sums up the philosophy you need to balance long-term vision with short-term endeavour.

Be clear about where you're going but flexible about how you get there.

WHAT TO DO IF YOU'RE STRUGGLING

Still struggling to define your values? Don't worry, this can be difficult, which is why you need to keep coming back to the question of what matters most. Some people might be crystal clear about their purpose, but, let's be honest, most of us aren't. However, cultivating meaning in our work/lives is important. Not only does it correlate with happiness, it positively impacts motivation, productivity and, ultimately, performance.

So, let's approach this from another angle. What might be preventing you from finding your purpose?

Could you be overcomplicating it?

Forget about identifying a worthy ideal and just focus on what you find interesting. We get so bogged down with the significance of 'discovering our purpose' that it often puts us off from even starting. Don't overthink it. Concentrate on things that you enjoy and make you feel good.

One approach I took was to use the Japanese idea of Ikigai – 'the reason for being'.

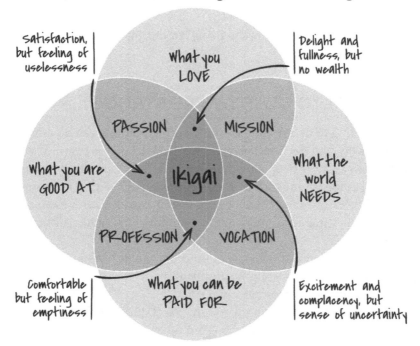

Ikigai
A Japanese concept meaning 'a reason for being'

Satisfaction, but feeling of uselessness

Delight and fullness, but no wealth

What you LOVE

PASSION

MISSION

What you are GOOD AT

Ikigai

What the world NEEDS

PROFESSION

VOCATION

Comfortable but feeling of emptiness

What you can be PAID FOR

Excitement and complacency, but sense of uncertainty

Although the concept itself doesn't translate literally into English, it has been popularized by a Venn diagram, which focuses on four elements that make up a meaningful life:

- What you're good at;
- What the world needs;
- What you can be paid for and; importantly…
- What you love.

If you're missing any one part, then it's likely you won't be completely satisfied. For example, combine the first three elements, and you'll probably be comfortable but unfulfilled.

When I went through the exercise of identifying my Ikigai in early 2020, the idea immediately resonated. I could see why I had the 'hollow' feeling about my work towards the end of the time at my company.

I was good at it, and I was getting paid well, but did I love it? No. Did the world need what I was creating? If it did, I didn't believe it. So, I did what anyone else would and got my Post-it notes out.

I drew the Ikigai diagram on a whiteboard (or in my case some Magic Whiteboard sheets — amazing stuff!) and started writing out my thoughts for each section, starting with the things I love:

> My family, music, reading, cooking, yoga, learning, working with young people, challenging myself with ideas that I struggle to understand and (maybe) cracking them, meal planning, going for long walks, collaborating in groups, football, spreadsheets, visiting new places.

Next, the things I think I'm good at:

> Selling stuff, cooking and eating well, teaching and coaching, empathizing, yoga, creating bedtime stories to tell my kids (most involving a character called Jammy Hurnard, but that's for another day…), motivating people, contextualizing business problems and creating solutions, working out ways to use tech to help improve efficiency and communication.

Yes, fair enough, I shoehorned the last few in there. That wasn't the full list, though, and the reality of this exercise is that your passions and hobbies can often sound a lot more natural than work skills.

I summarized the things I love and am good at into the following categories — creativity, communication, health and wellbeing, problem-solving.

A quick assessment told me that many of us could benefit from improving our health and wellbeing while simultaneously focusing on managing our time and communicating better. I understand what it takes to run businesses and teams and I'm great at solving problems. Plus, not only am I good at bringing out the best in others, I love it. Surely that's something people will pay for?

All of this led me to conclude that much as I was thinking about how to redesign my own work/life, I could help others do the same.

Two years later, here I am doing it!

SUMMARY

- Using The Code's simple framework can help you define your values.
- Commitment to anything requires pursuing the goal while ignoring the millions of other available opportunities.
- Non-negotiables force you to identify the things on which you'll never compromise.
- Establishing your 'north star' helps clarify where you're going, even while being flexible about how you get there.
- If defining your values is difficult, concentrate on where you already spend your time and what you find interesting.
- Ikigai – a meaningful life – requires combining what the world needs, what it will pay for, what you're good at and, importantly, what you love.

7

Prioritizing what matters

'What do you want to be when you grow up?' It's up there with 'are we nearly there yet?' in the most memorable phrases of our childhoods. In my case, I had a dream of one day driving my neighbourhood streets in an ice-cream van, sampling my wares as I went. Fortunately, no one pointed out to me at the time the role seasonality would play in my entrepreneurial ventures. Let alone what we know now about the proliferation of speed bumps, which, presumably, plays havoc with any mobile food-based business.

Nonetheless, my mum still tells this story, and unknowingly I've adopted this strange obsession with what job children want to have when they're older.

On the first day of every school year, my children create a sign, writing down their age, what class they're entering and, importantly, what they want to be when they grow up. For us parents, it's an endearing moment to capture in time and perfect for the grandparents' Christmas calendar gift. However, recently I've started to wonder what the question really tells us. What are the chances my daughter will be a pop star, or my son a professional footballer? Possible, I suppose, although unlikely given the odds. The reality is that whatever they write, and however mundane the job, you can rarely predict anyone's profession early in life. In fact, the idea of a 'profession' at all seems incredibly dated – a relic from a bygone era.

The more I think about it, the clearer I become that the question itself may not be wrong but our expectations about the answer certainly are. Rather than request my children pick out their future job, surely it's more important that we focus on our values and what we want to experience in our work/lives.

Perhaps a better answer to the question 'what do you want to be when you grow up?' would be something like:

- 'I want to be constantly learning.'
- 'I want to be challenged by my work every day.'
- 'I want to be someone that people turn to when struggling with the challenges life presents.'
- 'I want to be the reason why someone decides to stop being unhappy with the job they're stuck in and builds the courage to pursue their dreams.'
- 'I want to be happy and grateful for the life and relationships I have.'

With that in mind, once we've clarified our values, our priority should be making sure we follow through and spend our time on the right things.

THE FOUR-WAY VIEW

During the early days of COVID-19, like millions of other families around the world, our house was chaotic, to put it mildly. Forced to retreat to the security of a few rooms and, fortunately, in our case, a back garden, my wife and I did our best to shield the kids from the anxiety of neither knowing the seriousness of the virus' threat nor how long this new idea of a lockdown would last. With three young kids at home all day, every day, and two of them needing home-schooling, any illusion of work/life balance was shattered forever.

Fortunately, I'd just ordered a copy of Stew Friedman and Alyssa Westring's book, *Parents Who Lead*,[20] which promised to provide a blueprint on using the lessons we learn in business and applying them to family life. Perfect for a business book nerd like me.

'What have I got to lose?', I thought.

In a case of the right book at the right time, I discovered the framework they'd created to help people identify where they should be spending their time each day. The Four-Way View model emphasizes why an integrated approach to our work/life is the only realistic way to manage its complexity. Using the Four-Way View, you start examining whether you spend your time on the things you really care about and, crucially, how that aligns with other significant people in your lives.

Let me share it with you.

The first step is to visualize how your life will look in the future if you're able to live by the values that you identified in the last chapter. The trick here is to literally imagine the things you'll be doing as part of a happy, purposeful life.

In 15 to 20 years, say, what do you do when you wake up in the morning? Get out of bed and exercise? Meditate for half an hour? (Metaphorically) read the newspaper cover-to-cover? Roll over, snooze the alarm and go back to sleep? Open the doors out onto the garden and jump in the pool for a swim?

What are you doing during the day? Are you still doing the job you love today? Are you spending your morning on a hobby and then working in various advisory roles every afternoon? Are you volunteering? Have you finally taken that yoga teaching course?

And how does the end of your day look? Are you congregating for a family meal? Working on a series of passion projects? Dialling into conference calls for the international business that you own? Or are you sitting quietly with a book?

It's easy to get stuck in the moment without taking the opportunity to step back and get some perspective. Visualizing the future can be a

---

[20] Stewart D. Friedman and Alyssa Westring, *Parents Who Lead: The Leadership Approach You Need to Parent with Purpose, Fuel Your Career, and Create a Richer Life*, Harvard Business Review Press, 2020.

valuable and positive reminder of why we're doing 'this' now (whatever 'this' is).

Back in the present, you need to look objectively at how you're spending your time, which is where the four dimensions of your work/life come in:

- Yourself
- Your career
- Your family
- Your community

ARE YOU SPENDING YOUR TIME WHERE YOU SHOULD BE?

Here's an easy exercise you can do to determine how you'd spend your time in an ideal world and how you're doing right now:

1. Create a simple table, noting down the percentage of your waking hours that you'd like to dedicate to each of the four areas.
2. After spending 15 to 20 minutes reviewing your calendar, create another table in which you add how much time you *actually* spend on each.
3. If you have a partner, ask them to do this separately before comparing notes.

What's the objective?

- To assess whether you're meeting your time aspirations.
- To discover which parts of your life are getting more or less attention than they deserve (don't worry, if you're like 99% of people, you won't be anywhere near your intended split).
- To give you a starting point to begin designing your time differently.

To ensure you and your family are on the same page about your respective values.

This last part is essential because making big changes in your work/life is challenging, and you need the support of the people you care about.

For example, by using the techniques we've explored in this chapter and the previous one, I've identified my five non-negotiable values, which determine where I focus my energy:

- Autonomy
- Creativity
- Curiosity
- Growth
- Humour

As well as giving you insight into how you spend your time, this exercise may also reveal why you're not as satisfied in your career as you'd like. If you're spending more time at work than you'd like *and* you're in a job you're not enjoying, it's a recipe for misery.

So, take action now and start planning your future work/life.

FROM THE BALLROOM TO THE BIRTH ROOM

Carly Sandland has been through this process, and although it has not always been an easy journey, she has emerged with a renewed sense of purpose in her life.

When *she* grew up, she wanted to be an actress. She stuck with her dream for far longer than most of us too, accepting a place to study drama at university. However, soon after starting her degree, she began suffering from anxiety, manifesting in stage fright. Within weeks of starting her course, she felt under pressure to pick a different path and stumped for the closest thing she could find related to her dream job – media and communication studies.

As happens so often, one snap decision determined the course of Carly's life.

After graduation, she worked at an entertainment PR firm, before moving to a TV production company, where she met friends for life and who introduced her to her future husband. Her career continued building momentum, taking her in exciting directions, including working with some of the UK's top television and comedy talent, and culminating in her leading the communications strategy for hit primetime show *Strictly Come Dancing*.

> I got to work on some of the best British television there's ever been, and for most of my time at the BBC, I worked at the iconic Television Centre building. It was exciting and challenging at the same time.

Looking from the outside in, Carly appeared to have the perfect job, but she didn't feel like that. Whereas she saw colleagues as 'naturals, thriving in their roles', she never felt comfortable working in PR. Rather than satisfy her love of television and entertainment, her career was exacerbating her anxiety.

> I didn't like speaking to journalists because I found the crisis management side of it too uncertain. Plus, there were downsides to working on a prominent primetime BBC show. You were expected to be available 24/7.

She needed a change but didn't know how to take the next step.

Being made redundant shortly after returning to work following the birth of her first child, nudged her in the right direction. She initially took a short-term role at another television company, but this only confirmed that the time had come to reimagine her career. Although she didn't know what was next, she decided to spend her time following her curiosity and exercising her creative spirit.

Carly is not one to sit around doing nothing. While pregnant, she'd begun documenting her journey to becoming a mum in a blog that quickly became a popular read among her friends and other expectant and new mums. She also started volunteering to support other women breastfeeding their newborns and launched a baby skincare product.

For the first time in her life, she felt at home in the work she was doing, which gave a newfound sense of fulfilment.

She decided to continue learning, training to teach pregnancy yoga and antenatal and hypnobirthing, and became a doula, supporting women and their partners leading up to and during birth.

> It sounds cheesy, but I believe it's my calling. I'm so passionate about it and will talk about birth to anyone who'll listen!

Working on her own for the first time was tricky, but she has found a new community online through training courses and other birth workers she has met on social media. Crucially, she has also focused on experimenting with new ways to support her peers and clients, consistently sharing the lessons she has learned from her growing experience and research with followers online.

She has created a Work/Life Flywheel that aligns her purpose with her natural creativity and willingness to learn from her community.

It took Carly a while to generate a steady income, but her husband's job allowed her the time to make decisions that have led to her discovering where her passion, skills, and what the world needs overlap. Together they divide their time on the things that matter most to them.

Not that it's easy.

Like many dual-career couples with kids, operating under severe time constraints is difficult and can sometimes put a strain on their relationship. However, in a fantastic demonstration of teamwork, she's now able to support her husband as *he* undergoes his own career transition, showing what an incredible job she's doing, all while bringing up their three young children together.

Although I would say that. Carly's my wife.

SUMMARY

- The era of a 'profession for life' is over – instead, we should focus on our values and what we want to experience in our work/lives.
- The only way to manage its complexity is by taking an integrated approach to our work/life.
- The Four-Way View helps you do a time audit and check whether you're spending it in a way which aligns with your aspirations.
- Visualizing how your life will look in the future unlocks insights into how you manage your time now.
- Designing a Work/Life Flywheel helps you overcome the inevitable challenges of pivoting your career.

8

Visualizing your goals

S o, you've established what matters most and where you'd like to focus your time. Now you need to work out how to get there by setting goals.

How do you do it?

Well, it turns out most of us have been approaching goal-setting all wrong. There have been countless books written on how to set goals, usually accompanied by a handy acronym like the SMART model, which I learned early in my career. The letters, in this case, denote that each goal should be:

- **S**pecific
- **M**easurable
- **A**ttainable
- **R**epeatable
- **T**ime-bound

Not a bad start, but based on experience, five words aren't enough to guarantee success, which is partly why so many people struggle to achieve their objectives. So, if something's missing, how do you fill in the gaps? As you've probably worked out by now, my newly discovered attitude in life is to follow my curiosity and, in this case, I wondered who are the world's leading experts on goal-setting and whether they might be able to help us answer this question.

Enter Emily Balcetis.

Emily is a professor at New York University, where she runs the Social Perception Action and Motivation research lab – SPAM for short. She and her team have pioneered the scientific investigation of behavioural science and motivation, uncovering strategies that 'increase, sustain, and direct people's efforts to meet their goals'. It sounded to me like she could be the person to help us break this down, and I was right!

STARTING WITH THE END IN MIND

One fundamental discovery from the lab's work is that the secret to achieving and exceeding goals is to 'materialize' them – to see them as real-life things.

To do this effectively means visualizing the objective – either in your mind's eye or in your real eyes if you're a top-level athlete, which is where Emily's research began. After initially observing Olympic champion athletes train, Emily investigated where they focused their attention while running. In every case, the runners fixed on a single point in the near-distance. For sprinters, it was the finish line, whereas long-distance runners would track a competitor up ahead or a fixed point on the bend of the track.

Fixing their attention on a single point contracted their perception of distance, inducing a visual illusion that it was nearer.

You might say that that's all very well for world champion athletes, but what about us regular folk? Emily and her team felt the same, so they experimented with two groups of students. The objective was simple. Run between two points in the shortest time possible. They gave Group 1 no further instructions. On the other hand, they asked Group 2 to keep focusing on the finish line.

The result?

Group 2 experienced 17% less exertion and completed the activity 23% faster.

They were faster *and* the exercise took less effort. Simply by focusing on a point in the distance. What's more, the positive effect didn't just last the duration of the experiment. The group reported increased activity and performance levels for the full week afterwards.

So, how might we use these insights in our work/lives?

The obvious place to start is by applying these lessons using a narrow focus to help us exercise. Physical fitness enhances our performance in other areas of our lives, too, creating a complementary relationship with our work. Specifically, it improves our concentration, creativity and productivity.

However, we can also use the same approach to help set non-fitness-related goals.

Take this book, for example. Writing a book takes a long time. You need to research it, interview experts and contributors, and synthesize the information before eventually writing it. That's not the end of the process, though. Once you've written a draft, it needs editing and rewriting until it's ready for public consumption. A book of this length – around 50,000 words – takes months, if not years, to compile – trust me!

With such a distant target, the main challenge is recognizing the contribution of the work you do every day to the result – it just seems too far away. To visualize the goal means bringing it closer, or better put, splitting the goal into small pieces and tackling each in turn.

Temporal distance – the way we measure the dimension of time – directly affects our psychology. Since it's so difficult to connect our choices today with something that won't pay off until many years in the future, we often don't follow through on the goals we set. For example, it's notoriously difficult to get young people to save money for their futures, so experts like Emily have dedicated their efforts to understand how to change their behaviour.

Following Hal Hirschfield's work at the University of California, the SPAM lab ran an experiment to test the willingness of students to save each month for retirement.

Understandably, very few initially wanted to whittle down their spending money to create a more comfortable life in 50 years. That is until they saw a future version of themselves. Using computer visualization software, Emily and her colleagues superimposed aged versions of the students' faces onto successful figures from public life. Suddenly, they were seeing themselves in the future – or at least images close enough to what they might look like to make an impact. Their propensity to save increased when they could see themselves in the story.

FORESHADOWING FAILURE

One secret to enhanced motivation can, therefore, be to visualize yourself in the future.

If this sounds like something you might have heard before, you'd be right. The idea of positive visualization is nothing new. A 2016 TD Bank survey showed that at least one in five new entrepreneurs use vision boards to project their future success. However, when used in isolation, they can actually *reduce* your chances of achieving your goals.

Why?

Let me give you a quick science lesson.

When those athletes we were thinking about earlier step into the blocks at the start of a race, their systolic blood pressure – that's the number at the top if you've ever had one of those blood pressure armbands on – spikes. Their nervous system prepares them for action, priming their bodies for peak performance. The problem with vision boards is that they paint a rosy picture of success, tricking your brain into relaxing – it imagines you've already achieved your goal and your systolic blood pressure drops.

So what should you do?

The secret is pairing positive visualization with the ominous-sounding 'foreshadowing of failure'. Simply put, you have to plan for what could go wrong. What could prevent you from reaching your goals?

In legendary Olympian Michael Phelps' case, foreshadowing failure was a superpower.

He and his coach thought of every possible eventuality while preparing for races, so when his goggles filled with water only a few strokes into the 200m butterfly final at the 2016 Olympics, Phelps didn't panic. He'd been through this scenario numerous times in training, so he resorted to the back-up plan – counting his strokes. Despite swimming blind, he won one more of his 23 gold medals.

So, to maximize your chances of achieving your goals, you need to picture yourself in your ideal future without forgetting to consider the obstacles that might prevent you from getting there.

And remember, there's something in the idea of SMART goal-setting too.

Not least, being specific about how you'll judge success, and doing it *before* you start the process. Memories are notoriously unreliable, so you need to be clear about where you begin and where you're heading. Use objective milestones to measure how you're performing, and don't forget to review it! Tracking your progress, in a journal, for example, makes what you're doing concrete. Writing it down produces a visual manifestation of what could otherwise get lost in the messiness of our busy lives.

As Emily Balcetis writes in her book, *Clearer, Closer, Better:*[21]

> Notating our personal data makes us responsible to ourselves and our aspirations.

The other advantage of measuring how you're getting on is to ensure that you're heading in the right direction. Stepping back and applying a wide visual bracket allows you to judge whether the goals you're pursuing still align with your purpose.

Remember that Stephen Covey quote from Chapter 6? There's no point climbing the ladder if it's leaning against the wrong wall.

THE IMPORTANCE OF AIMING HIGH

On that note, now we know the importance of visualizing our goals, foreshadowing failure and setting clear markers to help us measure our progress, the next question is how high should we aim?

There's a difference between creating a list of daily or weekly tasks and identifying your life and career goals. Yes, your day-to-day work helps you get where you want to go, but how do you set that big target

---

[21] Emily Balcetis, *Clearer, Closer, Better: How Successful People See the World,* Ballantine Books, 2020.

to aim at? In fact, what's the point in even setting goals when plans so frequently change, and life can often feel uncertain?

As author and President of the Talent Strategy Group, Marc Effron, explained to me on the *Future Work/Life* podcast, the science is unequivocal – setting goals, specifically big ones, is a vital component of high performance at work.

It's human nature not just to live up to expectations but to exceed them. In some people, that manifests as proving people wrong – 'I'll show them'. In others, it comes from wanting to demonstrate that our parents, friends, partner or boss are right to believe in us. Lastly, some people are just intrinsically motivated to achieve their maximum, given the tools at their disposal.

In practice, our performance rises to the level of well-defined and appropriately judged goals.

As a track athlete with the ambition of competing for an Olympic title, you may have a particular target time in mind, which would make you a likely champion. Setting that big goal provides the discipline to stick with the strict diet and training regime and achieve your best. And like any other skill, you should treat goal-setting as something to improve on over time. Aiming high will help you do this.

Marc Effron's book *8 Steps to High Performance: Focus on What You Can Change (Ignore the Rest)*[22] gives a fantastic example of someone who achieved this to legendary effect.

While in the middle of a commission from Pope Julius II in 1506, Michelangelo, first and foremost a sculptor, was asked by the very same Pope to down his tools and pick up a paintbrush. The 'client' had decided he had other priorities and wanted the ceiling of the Sistine Chapel painted with an image of the twelve apostles.

After politely declining, initially, invoking his already busy schedule, Michelangelo eventually caved in on one condition. Instead of a relatively simple painting, he outlined a grand vision of illustrating major Old and New Testament stories in the form of hundreds of figures and powerful images. What's more, Michelangelo brought in a famous theologian and friend, Augustinian friar Giles of Viterbo, to advise him

---

[22] Marc Effron, *8 Steps to High Performance: Focus on What You Can Change (Ignore the Rest)*, Harvard Business Review Press, 2018.

on the project, reinforcing his already extensive biblical knowledge – this was the sixteenth-century, ecclesiastical equivalent of hiring Jony Ive (Apple's legendary chief designer) and Tim Cook (previously COO and now CEO) to plan and execute your new product launch!

We all know the result.

Julius (the Steve Jobs character in my fantastical and tenuous comparison) and Michelangelo knew what they were doing because, whether consciously or not, it was a textbook example of goal-setting.

The Sistine Chapel project demonstrated:

- **Alignment** – Michelangelo agreed with Julius' vision but suggested improvements.
- **A Promise** – he reprioritized his time and made the chapel his primary goal.
- **Increasing** the target by setting a stretch goal – why only paint a dozen people when he could create hundreds?
- **Framing** – Michelangelo and his client agreed on a specific, substantial and measurable goal – to create a masterpiece on the ceiling of the chapel.

While there's no precise formula for setting goals, follow the rules we've covered, and you'll significantly increase your chances of success.

Let's now turn to another vital skill that you'll need to nurture to achieve your ambitions: creativity.

SUMMARY

- Materializing your goals – seeing them as real-life things – increases your chances of meeting and exceeding them.

- Fixing your attention on a single point contracts your perception of distance, inducing a visual illusion that it's nearer.

- The secret to maximizing your chances of success is pairing positive visualization with 'foreshadowing failure'.

- Being specific about how you'll judge success in advance avoids being tricked by your unreliable memory.

- Setting objective milestones ensures you're always heading towards your 'north star'.

- Aiming high, and having people to help hold us accountable, pushes us to reach our potential.

Creativity

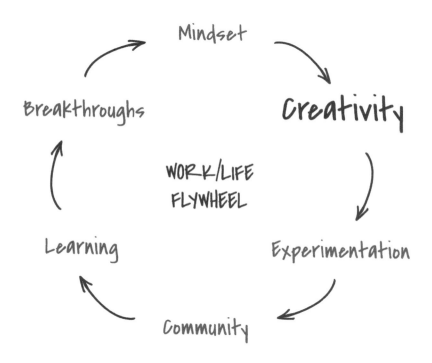

9

Creative magic

'**I**'m not very creative.'

After a childhood punctuated by various failures at learning to play instruments and scarred by an inability to progress beyond rudimentary stick people in art class at school, I didn't consider myself creative.

It wasn't until much later that I understood that creativity isn't something reserved for painting and music or writing poems or short stories. Instead, it manifests in manifold ways and differently for every individual. We can all be creative if we follow our curiosity and focus on things we genuinely care about.

Creativity has always been an important skill at work, but it's about to become the most significant of all.

As technology and automation change the nature of jobs over the coming decades, the defining contribution of humans to business and society will be characteristics like creativity, context and critical thinking.

As Lynda Gratton explained:

> Humans do two things that machines don't. They show high levels of empathy, and they listen. When you speak to a machine, it doesn't understand you. It's not empathizing with you. The second thing that humans can do is be creative, bring in new ideas, and make new connections.

For the time being at least, it seems unlikely that machines will be able to replicate our ability to make links between previously unconnected ideas.

Of course, creativity can mean many different things, but consider these three perspectives for inspiration.

- Leesman's Tim Oldman highlights the need to think afresh about the skills required in future workplaces, starting with leadership. Not least, 'applying historical skills to a whole new set of challenges and dialling up the creativity, to ensure "no" is not the first answer' to the difficult questions asked by people taking a more flexible approach to their work.
- Melissa Daimler, who has spent her career leading learning and development at companies like Adobe, Twitter and WeWork, is now Chief Learning Officer at online course business, Udemy. She explained to me how teams work creatively to develop a set of shared values, which ultimately help shape an organization's culture. With the location and mode of work changing, this becomes even more important as relationships adapt and evolve.
- In her former role as Director of Operations of Uber, venture capitalist Cleo Sham told me how they used viral video games to boost brand recognition and drive new registrations. Creativity is now one of the key attributes she looks for in founders, but it's not just about sales and marketing, although that helps. Entrepreneurs need to show how they think differently about solving problems by approaching them from new angles. As Cleo puts it: 'their ability to see around corners'.

So, to succeed in the future of work, you need to up your creative game.

The good news is that there are certain principles you can apply, which will give you a head start.

Over the next couple of chapters, we'll dig into the power of stories and flow state, and you'll learn how harnessing them will create momentum in your Work/Life Flywheel. Before then, let's explain why creativity is inherently good for you before focusing on how to channel it to generate value for others.

THE MAGIC OF CREATIVITY

In author Julia Cameron's bestselling creative guide, *The Artist's Way*, her number one principle is that:

> Creativity is the natural order of life. Life is energy – pure creative energy.

Nurturing a creative mindset is exciting.

When you wake up every morning knowing that you have the opportunity to produce ideas that no one has ever thought of in the same way, you've discovered a superpower. Or should I say *rediscovered* because when I watch my kids playing with their friends, they're constantly showing their creative spirit:

- Imagining there's a monster chasing them and retreating into a den made of cushions and blankets.
- Cooking up a meal of pasta and corn on the cob in their Ikea play kitchen.
- Celebrating a sweet volley into the corner of the goal in the garden as they picture themselves scoring in the World Cup final.

We're all creative, and capturing moments of magic in our everyday work/lives won't just unlock career success, it will provide moments of joy along the way.

Creativity is a state of mind and a willingness to think differently about problems and solutions. Author Annie Auerbach nicely summed up what happens when we connect the dots:

> Cross-connection may be the key to creativity... Smashing together two ideas which have not been connected – that is a breakthrough. That is what makes creative friction and sparks something fresh.[23]

---

[23] Annie Auerbach, *Flex: Reinventing Work for a Smarter, Happier Life*, HarperOne, 2021.

And it doesn't always show up in the most obvious of places, so we have to keep an open mind and our eyes peeled. Rory Sutherland shared a great example of this from a pilot on a flight he took into Gatwick airport. The plane taxied in but stopped with the terminal still in the distance. While his immediate thought was how tight the airline was to avoid paying for an airbridge, the pilot's voice came over the tannoy and immediately changed his perspective.

'I've got some bad news and some good news,' he said. 'The bad news is that another aircraft is blocking our arrival gate, so it'll have to be a bus. The good news is that the bus will drive you all the way to passport control, so you won't have to walk far with your bags.'[24]

RECOGNIZING THE CREATIVITY OF OTHERS

A creative lifestyle isn't just about what *you* do. It's about immersing yourself in the creativity of others, too, because this inspires action. I've seen this myself through my reading habits. As you'll know by now, I love reading business books, but unfortunately, this has led to periods over the past few years in which I've neglected fiction.

'No big deal', you might say. Well, it turns out it is.

Recent research from neuroscientists has shown that reading literary fiction builds empathy, improves critical thinking, and opens the mind more effectively to other viewpoints. It supports the development of in-demand skills which are typically hard to train – such as flexibility and adaptability, creative problem-solving, and judgement.

Never forget the value of transcending the here-and-now and seeing life through someone else's eyes.

Reading and social cognition – the process of perceiving other people and social situations – both tap into the default network, the

---

[24] Rory Sutherland, *Alchemy: The Dark Art and Curious Science of Creating Magic in Brands, Business, and Life*, Custom House, 2021.

part of the brain that supports our capacity to simulate hypothetical scenes, spaces, and mental states. An ability to keep an open mind improves decision-making. There is now overwhelming evidence of how people's propensity to resist what's called 'cognitive closure' allows them to be more thoughtful and creative, all of which contribute to higher emotional intelligence. People who depend on cognitive closure are more likely to struggle to change their minds as new information arises, and are less willing to produce alternative explanations or solutions to problems. They will also draw on a smaller pool of information and data, while their natural ability to consider other viewpoints is significantly reduced.

When framed through a story, it's easier to relate to the experience of others.

Away from the science, a well-written narrative is incredibly engaging and can persuade and inspire in fundamentally different ways from non-fiction, so you should consider this when designing your work/life. Optimizing for creative inputs and outputs will increase your empathy and decision-making ability. It also makes it easier to persuade other people, which is an invaluable skill when developing your career and building a business, I'm sure you'll agree!

To illustrate why that matters, let's consider one of the most creative groups of musicians ever formed – The Beatles – and why we shouldn't confuse our pursuit of creativity with one of modern work/life's most (in)famous ideas.

I ME MINE AND THE MYTH OF PERSONAL BRANDING

When The Beatles began recording their album, *Let It Be*, in 1969, the band was hanging together by a thread.

Six years after 'Beatlemania' catapulted them into superstardom, it's hardly surprising that the pressure had taken its toll. Guitarist George Harrison, still only 26, wrote the song, *I Me Mine*, during the recording sessions. Later, he explained that the song reflected revelations he'd had about his ego while on LSD. However, at the time, its title encapsulated the mood around the band perfectly – perceived self-interest and self-importance, which endangered the collective magic that had always been present within this high performing team.

Fortunately, however, The Beatles were pros. When crunch time came, they were able to put their egos to one side, all understanding their roles in helping to achieve a shared objective – *creating music that their fans loved.*

I thought about this story after chatting to bestselling author and podcaster Christopher Lochhead on the *Future Work/Life* podcast. Highlighting some of modern business's most troublesome ills, he told me:

> Personal branding is [a] source of intergalactic bullshit... The most legendary people become known for a niche or category they own, and the stupidest thing about 'hustle' is it perpetuates the myth that you and I make ourselves successful. We don't make ourselves successful. Other people do.

Personal branding has become a well-known phrase over the past decade, and its premise is that we as individuals should promote ourselves in the same way we would a pair of shoes or a packet of crisps. The problem with personal branding is that it's all 'I Me Mine'. It's become shorthand for making sure people can't miss you and know how great you are.

Unfortunately, in most cases, the advice also loses sight of why you're doing it in the first place. You should always ask yourself, what value are you generating for the people reading, watching or listening to what you're saying? Are you creating your equivalent of The Beatles' masterpiece, *Let It Be*, or are you more interested in receiving some easy 'likes' and virtual 'pats on the back'?

Remember: 'We don't make ourselves successful. Other people do.'

HUSTLE NO MORE

As for the idea we should 'always be hustling', it's easy to project the appearance of hyper-productivity to others. None of this is of any use, though, if you're not creating anything of value to yourself and, most importantly, others. These aren't new phenomena either. They've existed for millennia. Stoic philosopher Seneca described what we'd call 'the hustle' as 'busy idleness':

> All this dashing about that a great many people indulge in, always giving the impression of being busy.

Whether a Roman, a millennial, a boomer, or a zoomer, it's all too easy to get carried away by the productivity and self-improvement trends of the day. Stopping to get some perspective on the results of all that 'dashing about', on the other hand, is far trickier.

Psychologist and philosopher Erich Fromm distinguished genuine productivity, which requires careful thought and intentionality, from the more frenetic and scattered approach that typifies our modern definition – being active does not mean being busy but rather:

> It means to renew oneself, to grow, to flow out, to love, to transcend the prison of one's isolated ego, to be interested… **to give**.[25]

Ancient philosopher Aristotle advocated the concept of eudaemonia – or flourishing – which aligns neatly with Fromm's thinking. Being active means using our time and energy to grow and become a better person who gives more to others.

Christopher Lochhead summarizes the dangers of being too inward-looking by talking about the spread of 'Me Disease'. It isn't just that pursuing 'the hustle' or 'building your brand' wastes time. Worse than that, comparing yourself to others – and, in particular, a contrived social media version of others rather than the real thing – is bad for your mental health.

What's more, constantly focusing on yourself can be detrimental to personal growth. The posterior cingulate cortex (PCC) is a part of your brain that fires when focusing only on ourselves and our perspective. Just as there are neurobiological triggers for *entering* flow state, there are also *blockers*. Guess which part reduces the chances of getting into the zone? That's right, your PCC.

'Me Disease' is a neurobiological impediment to high performance.

---

[25] Erich Fromm, *To Have Or To Be?*, Harper & Row, 1976.

If you're concerned that you've been infected, take time to pause, step back and consider why you're doing what you're doing.

As with any aspect of your work, an easy starting point is to focus on the problem you're looking to solve or the opportunity you're creating for others. If that work involves posting insights or sharing advice on social media, that's fine, but the simple rule should be: Why should someone spend their time consuming it? What's in it for them?

And if you want something to compare yourself against, how about yourself – benchmark your health, creativity, or career success in terms of the progress you make in your work/life.

Author Annie Dillard once said that 'how we spend our days is how we spend our lives',[26] so please spend your day focusing on stuff that matters. For your sake and everyone else's.

Less *I Me Mine*, more *You Your Yours* and *We Us Ours*... or something like that.

With these lessons in mind, let's take a deeper look into flow and why its positive effects on our creativity and productivity are like pouring nitroglycerin into our Work/Life Flywheel.

——————————— **SUMMARY** ———————————

- Creativity has always been an important skill at work, but it's about to become the most significant of all.
- As technology and automation change jobs, human characteristics like creativity, critical thinking and context will be vital.
- Creativity is a state of mind and a willingness to think differently about problems and solutions.
- A creative lifestyle isn't just about what you do but also about immersing yourself in the creativity of others, which inspires action.
- An ability to keep an open mind improves your decision-making.
- Optimizing for creative inputs and outputs increases your empathy, decision-making, and ability to persuade others.
- Forget about personal branding and focus on the problem you're looking to solve or the opportunity you're creating for others.

---

[26] Annie Dillard, *The Writing Life*, Harper Perennial, 2013.

10

Find your flow

When Shaun Tomson found himself deep within 'the tube' – the part of a wave that barrels over, providing a momentary opportunity for only the most skilled and bravest surfers – his body, mind and the ocean were at one.

> I was known in surfing for creating a whole new style of riding inside the tube, which is the most exciting and dangerous part of the wave. You're rising inside this watery hurricane, inside this tornado of water. It's the most dangerous place because one mistake can mean a wipe-out, and then you can be smashed into the coral that's running right beneath you. I felt I could bend that wave to my will, man. I could slow down time. In some ways, you feel like you're a god. You feel like you're the master of that moment, and the exhilaration and power that you feel there, is unlike any other experience in life.

Once Mihalyi Csikszentmihalyi identified a name for the feeling that is both elusive and addictive, the idea of 'flow state' (flow) became etched into people's consciousness.

Descriptions of flow, like Shaun's, often lead us to picture high-performance athletes 'in the zone' or perhaps musicians or artists in an optimal state of creative concentration. However, as the neuroscience behind flow has become better understood, it's clear that harnessing it in any aspect of your work/life can provide exponential gains. Flow characterizes those moments in life during which we achieve complete concentration on a task. We have a heightened sense of awareness. Our sense of self vanishes, and our perception of time changes. Seemingly at once, time slows down, but hours disappear in minutes. We feel what Zen Buddhists call the 'paradox of control' – control without controlling.

The whole experience is intensely, intrinsically rewarding.

A journalist for most of his career, Steven Kotler has been fascinated by flow for 20 years. After observing and writing about action sports athletes who achieved record-breaking feats with little in the way of resources, he began exploring how reaching a flow state had propelled them to greatness. His obsession with discovering the roots of these performance gains led him to found the Flow Research Collective in 2019. His mission is to understand better how we can leverage flow's benefits to improve performance in all walks of work and life.

Is there a formula for bringing more flow into your life? While there's no simple 'hack', flow's neurobiological triggers are universal. As Kotler explains:

Personality doesn't scale. Biology does.

OPERATING UNDER CONSTRAINTS

I was initially so intrigued by flow because of the constraints I was increasingly operating under the more children I had. It turns out that life perfectly designed to maximize the effects of flow doesn't include broken nights of sleep punctuated by moments of high anxiety and stress throughout the day. When I first spoke to Steven Kotler, he didn't hold out much hope for me being able to maintain a life optimized for flow:

When it comes to having kids, you're kind of fucked.

Although he had his tongue planted in his cheek when he broke this to me, he was only half-joking.

The reality of life can often get in the way of high performance at work. No more so than when you have young kids. Nonetheless, I thought, I'm not the only person with responsibilities and demands on my time that restrict creating a 'perfect flow lifestyle'. And since flow state is a spectrum, I figured I could still benefit from some of the positive effects even if there were parts of my life that proved restrictive. Besides, if you can master the ability to drop into flow, you can do more in less time.

Why?

Research from Harvard University, the University of Sydney, McKinsey and DARPA has shown that you experience 500% improvements in productivity, 490% increases in learning speed and a 430% boost in creative problem-solving when in a flow state. In other words, it's a skill worth learning. So, what else is within my control that will compensate for the lack of recovery at night? And, if I could optimize in other areas, could I extract the benefits of achieving flow more consistently?

Well, it turns out you can. We just need to identify the right triggers.

22 FLOW TRIGGERS

The Flow Research Collective identify 22 flow triggers, broken down into four categories – internal, external, creative and social.

Think about each of the triggers as dials you can turn up. If all the dials are low, you get into flow, but it won't be too intense. However, as you start increasing the level of each, the deeper your experience of the state and its benefits will be.

So let's break them down:

Internal triggers:

1. Autonomy
2. The triad of curiosity, passion and purpose
3. Complete concentration
4. Clear goals
5. Immediate feedback
6. The challenge–skills balance

External:

    7. High consequences
    8. Novelty
    9. Unpredictability
    10. Complexity
    11. Deep embodiment

Creative:

    12. Creativity, including building a pattern recognition system, thinking differently and treating creativity as a virtue

Social:

    13. Complete concentration
    14. Shared, clear goals
    15. Shared risk
    16. Close listening
    17. Good communication
    18. Blending egos
    19. Equal participation
    20. Familiarity
    21. A sense of control
    22. Always say yes

Since social triggers focus on what's known as 'group flow' – our experience of working with others – we'll return to these in a future chapter. For now, let's concentrate on how developing our ability to enter a flow state individually helps realize gains in productivity, learning rates and, crucially, creativity.

INTERNAL TRIGGERS

Combining intrinsic motivations with the autonomy to choose when and how we do our work improves our attention and focus.

When we're in charge of our mind (freedom of thought) and our destiny (freedom of choice), our whole being gets involved. So, continually returning to the exercise of clarifying what we're deeply interested in, passionate about *and* why we're doing it is vital. As you think about the various tasks you work on during the week, start reflecting on how much they represent each of these three elements of intrinsic motivation.

You'll see that the more each of the three variables shows up, the easier it is to focus and perform at your best.

As you'll have noticed, complete concentration shows up both as a flow trigger and an output, which means you need to design your workspace to avoid distractions, whether these are emails, instant messaging, phone calls, or other multi-tasking temptations. There's a whole other book on how best to design your work/life to avoid distraction – just ask Nir Eyal, who wrote the excellent *Indistractable* – but the simplest methods, I've found, use this simple three-step checklist:

1. Can you achieve everything you need with a pen, some paper, and/or a single browser window or app?
2. Have you told everyone who might need to contact you that you're unavailable unless it's an emergency?
3. Have you placed all unnecessary devices out of reach or in another room?

In an ideal world, you'll create a 90–120 minute period without interruption. While this may initially feel difficult to imagine and justify (to yourself and others), consider the outcome. When done consistently and focused on the right things (which is where *clear* goals come in), combined with honest feedback from others, the uplift in performance means you'll deliver *more high-quality work in less time.*

If you doubted how impactful living a high-flow lifestyle is, that last sentence should have changed your mind!

However, achieving these improvements relies on one crucial factor – the *challenge–skills balance.* Finding the right level between the challenge of the task at hand and your *perceived* ability to do it is by far the most important flow trigger of all. So, what's the right balance, and how do we measure it?

Sure enough, there is a magic number – we pay most attention and increase the likelihood of entering flow when the challenge of the task is *4% harder* than our skillset.

If that seems impossibly specific to you, I felt the same. How on earth are we supposed to design our work so it's *precisely* 4% harder than our current skill level? Well, for starters, you can never achieve perfection, so the easiest way to think about this principle is always to aim to be stretched but not snap. If the task's too easy, we get bored. Too complex, and we get anxious.

Remember, the overall objective here is to improve performance, and much the same way as you get your Work/Life Flywheel turning, the way to achieve this is by progressing a little more each time.

EXTERNAL TRIGGERS

When the level of risk is elevated, you create the optimal conditions for flow. That's why you've probably experienced flow during an important meeting or presentation. Or perhaps when you've taken an exam or are completing work to a tight deadline. Because the stakes are high.

As Harvard psychiatrist Ned Hallowell explained in Steven Kotler's book *The Rise of Superman:*[27]

> To reach flow, one must be willing to take risks. The lover must bare his soul and risk rejection and humiliation to enter this state. The athlete must be willing to risk physical harm, even loss of life, to enter this state. The artist must be willing to be scorned and despised by critics and the public and still push on. And the average person – you and me – must be willing to fail, look foolish, and fall flat on our faces should we wish to enter this state.

The possibility of something unexpected around the corner – novelty – and the feeling of unpredictability can force the brain to switch on and focus.

---

[27] Steven Kotler, *The Rise of Superman: Decoding the Science of Ultimate Human Performance*, Quercus, 2015.

Likewise, complexity can be a positive factor, although this time, the trigger comes from the external environment rather than reflecting an increase in task difficulty. Breaking free of the usual routine, say, or working in a completely new setting. A different location forces your brain to expand its perceptual capacity – the amount of information we can take in at any one time.

If you can't actually base yourself somewhere else, don't worry, you can also achieve similar results by preceding the session by taking a walk in nature or reading something that broadens your perspective. The point is, a change of scene really makes a difference. *Variety* is the spice of life after all. And no more so than when it comes to the brain, as it introduces more of the neurobiological chemicals that help you enter flow (although, admittedly, that idiom loses something of its snappiness when it comes to neurobiology).

Talking of idioms, I always found the idea that you could 'sink your teeth into something' a little odd, particularly after spending six months trying to deter my toddler from doing that very thing to other children in his vicinity. However, in the context of the deep embodiment flow trigger, this kind of works, as when you're able to engage each of your senses, you become completely immersed in the task. During these moments, we reduce our cognitive load, connect more deeply to our bodies, and detach ourselves from the 'thinking mind'. Typically, this might involve an experience like gardening, or surfing for that matter. If you're wondering how to achieve the same result while sitting in front of a computer screen writing a report or before stepping into an important presentation, don't worry, there's a decent workaround. Mindfulness.

Deep embodiment is all about being in the moment. By paying close attention to your breath, you also become more aware of sound, touch, sight and smell, replicating the effects of a more physically sensory experience.

CREATIVE TRIGGERS

As we explored in Chapter 9, creativity is first and foremost about noticing connections between things in new ways.

Another notable feature is the courage to achieve creative results consistently and share those ideas with others. All of which rely on having a large bank of knowledge from which to draw. Designing your work/life to allow for ongoing learning gives you the toolkit to approach problems from new angles. Combine this with what we've learned about the importance of novelty and varying the physical environment in which you work, and you create the conditions for incredible creativity!

With all of this in mind, rather than considering creativity as a process or something appearing sporadically in life, it's better thought of as a value.

When I last interviewed Steven Kotler, he summarized this beautifully.

> Life should be art. Everything should be a creative decision. Creative decisions are all about mastery and excellence, and beauty.

We've now explored the importance of establishing the intrinsic motivators that allow you to unlock more creativity and learning in your work/life. The next question is how can we use stories to help understand ourselves and engage others?

Let's find out.

SUMMARY

- Flow state isn't something reserved for sportspeople or artists, you can harness it in your work/life.
- Everyone's habits and schedules may be different, but we all access flow in the same way.
- By getting into flow we significantly increase our creativity, productivity and rate of learning.
- Internal triggers require us to be in control, remove distractions, set the right goals and challenge level, and tap into our intrinsic motivation.
- Unpredictability, novelty and taking risks can help increase flow.
- Constant learning is a prerequisite to living a creative life, full of flow.

11

Telling stories

The smell of stewed coffee and baked beans is overwhelming. Every sense is pummelled. Snotty kids roam wildly across the café, flicking what's left of their dinner at each other. They're screaming at the top of their voices. Their parents have presumably abandoned them to complete the weekly 'big shop' at this identikit supermarket on the outskirts of an equally ordinary commuter-belt town.

I can feel the tears welling up. 'Stop it', I tell myself. But I can't.

The emotion stirring inside me is something I've never felt before, but the love of my life has never told me that she's leaving and that we won't see each other again. I feel crushed. We spend every moment in each other's company.

All those memories we've created together.

Running down the Welsh beach, frolicking in the waves and catching crabs.

Long, romantic walks in the woods, soaking up those rare moments of freedom from the pressure of daily life.

Sharing ice-cream direct from the tub as we watch one of our favourite movies together.

Can this really be it? If so, what does it mean for me? The future looks bleak.

Just then, my mum walks into the café. I wipe my eyes just in time. I don't think she notices and I'm relieved. How can I explain this to her?

It seems I don't need to.

'I saw Lucia's mum in the park earlier', mum says. 'She told me she's starting her new school in September. I'm sorry, I know you two are fond of each other.'

'Fond of each other', I blurt out, 'I love her and I'm never going to see her again!'

What a sight I look. An 11-year-old boy in a dirty football kit that's two sizes too big, sobbing into a plate of now soggy toast covered with Tesco own-brand beans.

'That's a bit of an exaggeration, Ollie', mum helpfully points out. 'You'll still see Lucia in the village. Anyway, you'll soon move on, you'll see.'

Thirty years later, I may indeed have moved on from my undying love for Lucia, but that moment is etched in my brain.

And the chances are you'll remember that sad image of my adolescent face more than most of the content in this book. Why? Because, among a sea of examples of people embracing the opportunities that come with reimagining their career, I've shared an incongruous story that captures a brief moment in time – when Lucia broke my heart.

THE POWER OF STORIES

Paul Zak is a neuroeconomist. He researches everything from positive traits like trustworthiness, generosity and sacrifice to negative ones like evil, vice and conflict. Most relevantly to us, though, he has also found some fascinating insights about how stories affect our brains and memory. To summarize, when someone uses character-driven stories with emotional content to illustrate their point of view, you're significantly more likely to remember it. Not just immediately afterwards but weeks later.

Stories engage us in the moment and are the most effective tool to get your point across and make it stick.

Paul Zak identifies three crucial characteristics of a good story well told:[28]

---

[28] https://hbr.org/2014/10/why-your-brain-loves-good-storytelling

1. Quickly develop tension.
2. Share the characters' emotions.
3. Focus on a single important idea.

Achieve all three, and you'll sustain your audience's attention and make your point heard.

He illustrated the effects of this in an experiment in which he asked participants to watch an emotionally charged film about a father and son. The story shares how the father feels watching his son playing, knowing that he's terminally ill and doesn't have long to live. I've watched an animated version of the video and I had a physical reaction to it despite knowing full well that it was designed for the experiment! It really is amazing.

Across the study, Zak and his team identified two neurochemicals it produced in viewers:

1. Cortisol left people feeling distressed and focused their attention on the story.
2. Oxytocin created a feeling of connection and empathy towards the father and son.

Interesting results in themselves, but not as significant as the outcomes they measured in a follow-up test. The researchers found that the people taking part in the experiment were more likely to give away money, whether to individuals they'd never met or unnamed charities. What's more, the level of oxytocin released predicted *how much* money – the more oxytocin, the more money they gave away. The narrative affected behaviour by changing people's brain chemistry.

As the late, great actor, Alan Rickman – he of the baddie in *Die Hard* and Professor Snape fame – said beautifully:

It's a human need to be told stories. The more we're governed by idiots and have no control over our destinies, the more we need to tell stories to each other about who we are, why we are, where we come from, and what might be possible.

HOW TO USE STORIES TO REIMAGINE YOUR CAREER

While I'm sure you recognize the value of stories by now, you might be wondering how this specifically relates to your decisions about changes you're making in your career.

Alan Rickman's last point is critical. Stories help explain what's possible, which matters when talking about something someone else cares about. You might be addressing a child, a partner, a client, or a colleague, but it could just as easily be yourself too.

We all have a personal narrative – a story that defines the key moments in our lives and what's next in our journey. Too often, these stories are negative and hold us back. To reimagine your career, you must first address *why* you want a change before crafting the story to help you achieve it.

Acknowledging the experiences and emotions that have shaped who you are is crucial if you want to understand what influences your decision-making. Start by being honest with yourself and those close to you about what's motivating you to change your work/life and what might be holding you back. Tell yourself your own story, starting with how you came to this point and what the future will look like for you. You don't need to kid yourself. You only have to be honest about your worries, hopes and what you believe in.

Next, consider your work story.

What's held you back in your career so far, and how are you overcoming these obstacles? As you reimagine your career, what does the next phase look like? How will you prioritize your time, and how will you feel as you begin making progress towards your goals?

The starting point with any story is to be honest, but to be truly effective, you have to be specific about the new future you're trying to create and bring it to life.

If you go back to Emily Balcetis' work on materializing goals, you'll remember that producing a destination in our mind's eye is the shortest route to stimulating change. Tell your story about what your future looks like, how you and other people will feel and what that feeling will empower you to do.

These storytelling principles don't end with visions of ourselves, of course.

The ability to communicate effectively helps you build credibility and inspire others. But you have to speak specifically to *them* and *their* problems. For a story to work, you must demonstrate you understand what it's like to be in the other person's shoes before showing them exactly how you'll help them create a brighter future. By mastering storytelling skills, you create powerful new possibilities in articulating your ideas and persuading others to join you on your mission.

The greatest stories in human history show moments of profound change – we start as one version of ourselves and end as something new. Redesigning your work/life is your opportunity to transform.

HOW TO TELL YOUR STORY

The Moth is a New York-based non-profit dedicated to the art and craft of storytelling.

Some legendary storytellers have stood on the stage at The Moth's events and shared incredible tales with millions of people watching and listening to their content. Possibly the best known of them all is Matthew Dicks. He's a Moth legend, having won their Grand Slam event five times. As he says in his book, *Storyworthy:*[29]

True stories are told by the people who live them.

I'm going to guess what you're thinking now. You're probably wondering why anyone would want to hear *your* story. You might be racking your brain for something interesting that you could share with people but are coming up short. Honestly, this is the most normal reaction in the world. Very few of us instinctively believe we've lived a life that people would be fascinated to hear about. Aside from narcissists, but then it's unlikely they bought this book.

---

[29] Matthew Dicks, *Storyworthy: Engage, Teach, Persuade, and Change Your Life through the Power of Storytelling*, New World Library, 2018.

In reality, though, people are interested in stories they can relate to, which means they *will* be interested in yours.

So, if our stories are so important, how do we capture them? How can we craft a story whenever we need it, to help motivate ourselves and others? Well, it just takes work – a consistent, structured approach to collecting stories.

Aside from the fact that Matthew Dicks can tell a good yarn, his book resonated with me because it articulated the value of a habit I'd developed far better than I ever could have done. Feeling increasingly like the days merged into one, in 2021, I added something to my daily journaling practice. As well as making a short note of daily highlights before bed each night (more on this in Chapter 18), I began recording one or two 'notable' stories or events that happened during the day. I'd occasionally return to this list and experience a magical feeling of being transported back in time to that moment. For years, I'd felt like I couldn't remember big chunks of my kids' childhood and here was a way to capture it. I found it improved my memory – amazing!

Matthew Dicks employs a similar approach but with a snappy name – 'Homework for Life'.

'Homework for Life' involves capturing what he calls 'story-worthy' moments and logging them digitally – in a spreadsheet or note-taking app. The practice allows you to start spotting recurring themes, which can trigger new ideas or, on the contrary, stop you from repeatedly making the same mistakes. Creating an external memory bank for significant moments in your life can also be the source of inspiration for stories, whenever you need it.

However, there's one standout benefit of employing this approach, whether it's Dicks' digitized version or writing it down in a journal, and here's what I couldn't previously explain: my sense of time has changed. Whereas life has increasingly felt like it's flashing by before my eyes, documenting significant and memorable events has created a feeling that time is slowing down.

I can remember every day in my life.

It's a revelation!

FREE-WRITING

There's one more technique that I'd love you to try.

I've experimented with 'free-writing' ever since I began picking up a pen and tapping on a keyboard again in 2020, but once again, Dicks has a more colourful and intentional way of leveraging this incredible technique. The basic idea behind free-writing is to start without any preconceived notions of what you want to achieve and jot down whatever comes into your head. Dicks calls this 'dreaming at the end of your pen'. By recording every memory that emerges within ten minutes, you'll recall events that you haven't thought about for years.

Good or bad, these are likely the stories that have formed your personality and beliefs. They present opportunities for you to contextualize decisions you make in the future, including how to influence others to join you on the next stage of your journey.

Matthew Dicks summarizes what differentiates a story-worthy moment from something forgettable. They're the occasions in life when something fundamentally changes you, and often take as little as five seconds.

It sounds rare, but they happen more often than you think.

In fact, if you adopt this habit, you've experienced one *just now*!

There's one indisputable fact about your life – you're the only one living it. Having more agency over the direction it takes requires you becoming the author of your own story. By slowing down and capturing some of these unique moments, you can begin to craft stories that help you define your future and carve out your unique niche.

And niches is where we turn to next.

SUMMARY

- Using character-driven stories with emotional content to illustrate your point of view makes it significantly more memorable.

- To reimagine your career, you must first address why you want a change, before crafting the story to help you achieve it.

- To be truly effective, you have to be specific about the new future you're trying to create and bring it to life.

- The ability to communicate effectively helps you build credibility and inspire others.

- You create powerful new possibilities in articulating your ideas and persuading others to join you on your mission by mastering storytelling.

- Recording 'story-worthy' moments allows you to spot trends in your thinking, trigger new ideas and slow down time.

- Free-writing enables you to recall stories from your past that have helped form your personality and beliefs, helping contextualize decisions you make in the future.

Experimentation

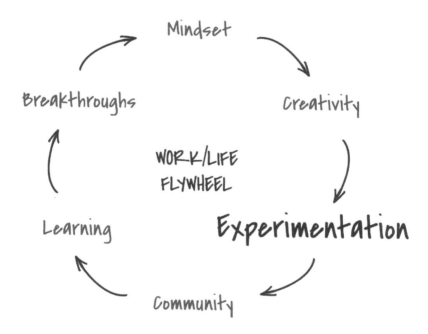

Mindset

Breakthroughs

Creativity

WORK/LIFE
FLYWHEEL

Learning

Experimentation

Community

12

Niching down

If creativity is now the most valuable skill in your toolkit, writing is arguably the most effective way of wielding it.

As soon as asynchronous work – people collaborating in different places at varying times – became commonplace during COVID-19, it was like a lightbulb lit up for millions worldwide. Not only can you get more done when you're working on your own in a distraction-free environment, but you can now work for any organization, anywhere in the world. Yes, there are times when you need to sync up with colleagues and clients, but these are far less frequent than we'd previously have acknowledged.

Asynchronous work has unlocked new levels of flexibility, but it also demands new, improved communication skills, and first among them is the ability to articulate your message through writing clearly.

Nicolas Cole – Cole, to anyone who knows him – is a writing pioneer. He's a digital writer who is not only comfortable communicating online but has built an incredibly successful career doing so. When he was 17, Cole was a professional World of Warcraft (WoW) player – yes, that is a real job – and documented his experiences to share with other WoW nuts. So began a journey that characterizes the internet's opportunities for aspiring creators and entrepreneurs.

As almost the entire world's population is now online, the scale of the potential audience for your product, service or ideas is limitless.

After moving on from sharing his teenage gaming stories, Cole graduated from college and went to the next level of digital writing.

He set himself the challenge to respond to questions on the social question-and-answer website Quora every day for one year.

By developing consistency and refining how he created value for questioners, he gradually became a go-to expert in his niche. When I say an expert, what I mean is he became Quora's top writer, racking up over 100 million views of his writing. That's tens of millions of people who read his work and recognized his unique take on the challenges they were experiencing.

With mass digital connectivity, the rules have changed, and we've all got the opportunity to engage our 'tribe' if we approach the process with discipline and learn lessons from the best – like Cole.

HOW TO GET STARTED

It's all very well bigging up the size of the possibilities at our fingertips. It's another thing entirely to make it work.

There are pros and cons to the internet. One of the downsides of social media is that there's a permanent record of everything you do. On the other hand, you can learn how others have achieved success. And there's a vital place to start because unless you know why you're doing it, you'll never be able to measure your progress.

So:

- What do you want to achieve?
- What's the perfect outcome?

As we saw in Chapter 8, it takes time to reach our objectives, but with the right approach, anything's possible. In the case of digital writing, you have the opportunity to use the internet to achieve unimaginable scale and can also rapidly test and iterate your ideas.

But if it's such a great opportunity, why do so few people do it?

Just as most people are afraid of making big changes in their careers, they're also afraid of putting themselves out there online. As Cole explained to me when we spoke on the *Future Work/Life* podcast:

The fear is rooted in expectation over the result. So if you expect approval, you're afraid you're not going to get approval. Or if you expect the first thing I write should make me money and it doesn't make you any money, the fear is I'm going to invest this time, and I'm not going to get any money. So for me, I always like asking people from the very beginning, why do you want to write? You have to be honest with yourself – why are you doing what you're doing?

Cole's writing career continued to develop as he spent more hours understanding the craft and focused relentlessly on the value he brought to the people reading his work. As he did so, he became a man in demand. Corporate leaders started to come to him to ask him to ghost-write articles and books for them, which eventually led him to create his business, Digital Press. He didn't stop there. Teaming up with Christopher Lochhead and Eddie Yoon, he launched *Category Pirates*, a paid for, long-form newsletter. He then created *Ship 30 for 30* with Dickie Bush, a cohort-based course for people to start building a digital writing habit. To date, 18 months later, 4,000 people have already taken the course.

Those 4,000 people are evidence that identifying a niche – helping people start writing digitally – can be simultaneously profitable while also representing a tiny proportion of total internet users.

As the saying goes, the riches are in the niches because:

> We have a flawed understanding of how many people there are in the world with a specific problem and how easily the internet can connect the right people to the right problems and the right solutions.

With no-code technology and apps providing cheap and easy tools to do everything from publishing content and analysing audience engagement to creating courses and collecting payment, it has never been easier to produce a digital product. Cole's a great example of someone who has made small bets over the years – such as ebooks on bodybuilding and digital writing – which continue to pay off today. Being known for something specific makes you the go-to person whenever someone needs that problem solved, so embrace it!

The same principles of niching down apply away from digital writing, particularly when launching a new business, pivoting your career, or reimagining how you can communicate your ideas and grow your community.

As Cole's writing partner, Christopher Lochhead, says in his book *Niche Down*:[30]

> Most of us are tricked into believing that achieving personal and professional success means fitting in. What it really takes is the courage to stand out.

COMBINING YOUR CAREER WITH YOUR PASSION

Fifteen years ago, Phil Askew had reached a transition point and needed to make a change.

His career had progressed well, taking him from a series of increasingly more senior graphic designer roles before becoming Creative Director of a successful agency. He loved the creative freedom the job offered him, but since he had no desire to run an agency, there was no further opportunity for career progression.

So what next?

To help him work this out, he went to see a coach, and in a now-familiar story, the impact it made helped him decide that he too wanted to help people navigate changes in their work/lives. A decade on, Phil had established a reputation as a coach of coaches – he became the go-to guy for coaches looking to advance their expertise and training. Yet, once again, he was having a wobble. He felt like something was missing.

On reflection, he realized he wasn't following his own advice.

Over time, he'd become fascinated by Ikigai, and as we know from exploring the idea in Chapter 6, identifying your reason for getting out of bed in the morning relies on aligning four things – what the world is willing to pay for, what the world needs, what you're good at and what you love.

---

[30] Christopher Lochhead and Heather Clancy, *Niche Down: How to Become Legendary by Being Different*, 2018.

As Phil explained:

> I'm spending five, six days a week coaching and building my practice, which does fulfil me to some degree, but there's no sense of creation by way of my own hand. I'm working in a relationship with others, which gives me a deep sense of meaning and fulfilment, but I'm not being creative.

Creativity was literally his job for many years, but he'd parked his natural curiosity with it as he established his coaching business and expertise. He had his 'a-ha' moment only after walking himself through the Ikigai process that he'd typically use with clients.

> I love photography, and I love taking photos of people, but I wasn't doing it at all. That's when I made the decision to incorporate it into my work. I didn't know how I was going to synthesize it at that time, but by blending it with mentoring, I realized I could put the two together to help my clients see themselves better. To be more visible and have a voice.

Like any pivot – business or career – the decision came with a degree of risk.

Combining coaching with portrait photography was not 'a thing'. It took time to establish whether it was even what people wanted. Phil was carving his niche, which inherently means creating new demand. If something doesn't exist, it's hard to put a price on it, which in the early days was a problem. Would people be prepared to pay the cost of two services when they were only used to paying for one?

However, with patience and persistence, Phil found that his unique offering started creating new opportunities rather than competing in a competitive market. His communication skills and photos' visual power have allowed him to develop a proposition that excites his customers and, crucially, himself.

Phil isn't the only person I've encountered who has successfully niched down. It characterizes the most successful solopreneurs and entrepreneurs I've interviewed as research for this book and many leaders within larger organizations too. Being known for something specific is a career accelerant, and when you connect that with something you're genuinely interested in, it's a recipe for fulfilment and growth.

Here are three more great niches I've come across:

- Former podcast guest, Bernhard Kerres, started life as a successful opera singer. He later became a technology executive before returning to his roots to run the Vienna Concert House as CEO and Artistic Director for six years. He has now found his niche, coaching professionals in 'Musical Group Coaching' that incorporates live classical musicians.
- I interviewed Ben Legg, CEO of the Portfolio Collective, a community for people pursuing a portfolio career, including one man who combined his love of drones with his legal training, to become the world's leading drone lawyer.
- In the birth worker world, in which my wife, Carly, is now immersed, there are some fabulous examples of people providing niche offerings, including marketing and social media coaching for 'birth babes'.

HOW TO NAME AND CLAIM YOUR NICHE

Here's how Cole and Dickie walk people through the process of naming and claiming their writing niche in *Ship 30 for 30*. You can use the same approach for any business or creative idea.

Step 1: Choose your topic: It could be education, wellbeing, technology, coaching, marketing or haberdashery.

Step 2: What (specifically!)? Ask yourself the question three times. Let's use careers as an example:
Version (V) 1: Careers
V2: High-Performance Careers
V3: Designing High-Performance Careers
Step 3: Who (specifically!)? Who are you doing it for? Again, ask yourself three times:

V1: Designing High-Performance Careers for Founders

V2: Designing High-Performance Careers for First-Time Founders

V3: Designing High-Performance Careers for First-Time Founders with Young Kids

Step 4: Why (specifically!)? Why does it matter to your potential audience or customers? What do they get from it?

V1 (Why?): Designing High-Performance Careers for First-Time Founders with Young Kids

V2 (Why, specifically?): Designing High-Performance Careers for First-Time Founders with Young Kids Who Want To Grow Their Business

V3 (Why, specifically?): Designing High-Performance Careers for First-Time Founders with Young Kids Who Want to Grow Their Business by Developing the Skills to Share Their Ideas with the World, But Are Short on Time

If you look at the two value statements below, one definitely jumps out more than the other:

- I write about careers.
- I write about designing high-performance careers for first-time founders with young kids, who want to grow their business by developing the skills to share their ideas with the world, but are short on time.

Going niche feels uncomfortable at first.

'Surely there aren't enough people interested in something so specific', you'll think to yourself.

However, as journalist and author Derek Thompson shared on the *Masters in Business* podcast:

People who want to be big sometimes think, 'I have to immediately reach the largest possible audience.' But in a weird way, the best way to produce things that take off is to produce small things. To become a small expert. And the reason why I think this is true I call my Tokyo example.

If you go to Tokyo, you'll see there are all sorts of really, really strange shops. There'll be a shop that's only 1970s vinyl and like, 1980s whisky or something. And that doesn't make any sense if it's a shop in a Des Moines suburb, right? In a Des Moines suburb, to exist, you have to be Subway. You have to hit the mass-market immediately. But in Tokyo, where there's 30–40 million people within a train ride of a city, then your market is 40 million. And within that 40 million, sure, there's a couple thousand people who love 1970s music and 1980s whisky.

The internet is Tokyo. The internet allows you to be niche at scale.

Experiment to find your niche but remember you don't have to stick with it for the rest of your life. The secret is to find something that resonates with you and the people you're talking to, which will require some testing.

--------------------------- **SUMMARY** ---------------------------

- Writing is one of the critical skills for the future of work.
- The scale of the online audience for your product, service or ideas is limitless.
- Digital writing allows you the opportunity to rapidly test and iterate your ideas.
- No-code technology means it has never been easier to produce a digital product.
- The secret to success as a digital writer, launching a new business or pivoting your career, is carving a niche.
- Being known for something specific is a career accelerant, particularly when combined with something you're genuinely passionate about.
- Going niche feels uncomfortable, but, by experimenting, you'll find something that resonates with you and your audience.

13

Designing tests

The chances are that at some point in your career, a fear of failure has stopped you from pursuing an idea.

Since redesigning my career in 2020, I've purposefully forced myself out of my comfort zone, repeatedly attempting new challenges in which I have no background and, arguably, no qualifications. Or at least, that is what I convince myself. That seed of doubt which lingers inside us can potentially be crippling and prevent us from progressing in our career and making positive decisions about work and life.

The reality is that most of us suffer from something similar, particularly when we're trying something new or attempting something unproven.

Having interviewed so many incredibly bright and successful people, what's reassuring is the honesty with which many of these folks approach subjects like imposter syndrome. Not with a sense of denial but rather a realistic perspective that breeds humility and an appreciation of how others can support our ambitions.

Take Glenn Elliott, for example.

After ten years as a software engineer at BT, he left to go it alone. He ran his design and marketing agency for seven years but eventually realized two things: consultancies are challenging to scale, and he didn't think he was a very good consultant anyway! His next business, on the other hand, proved far more successful. Over 12 years as CEO, he and his team grew Reward Gateway to over 400 staff servicing over 2,000 clients from six offices in the UK, Bulgaria, the USA and Australia. He sold the company to private equity on three occasions, eventually exiting entirely in 2021.

You might think that selling your business multiple times for a combined value of over half a billion pounds would be enough to reassure you of your capabilities and standing in the world of business.

Not for Glenn. He told me that he still experiences imposter syndrome every day. No more so than when he was asked to mentor a team of young executives at the private equity firm for which he's now Entrepreneur-in-Residence. He spent the next week googling 'tips for mentors'. However, he also explained that imposter syndrome isn't incompatible with the vision and drive required by successful entrepreneurs. It wasn't that he ever doubted that the market needed a new solution, nor that Reward Gateway provided it. He was just aware of his limitations, which tempered any overconfidence.

In his book, *Alive At Work*,[31] Dan Cable discussed the concept of 'humble leadership', which works by recognizing that no one's perfect and that the only path to success is through experimentation, learning, failing and improving. Cable writes about a study conducted by David Hekman at the University of Colorado. Following in-depth interviews with leaders from a wide variety of contexts:

> They found that when leaders express feelings of uncertainty and humility and share their own developmental journeys, they end up encouraging a learning mindset in others.

Why is learning so important in this case? Well, if you accept that you're always learning, it makes failing not just acceptable but necessary. I suggested to Glenn Elliott that he must have developed a trusted environment and close-knit team to be able to occasionally fail and accept that it's not always possible to get it right first time. Glenn went further, telling me that:

---

[31] Daniel M. Cable, *Alive at Work: The Neuroscience of Helping Your People Love What They Do*, Harvard Business Review Press, 2019.

It's not even failing occasionally; it's failing regularly. If you're only failing occasionally, you're not being that innovative. Innovation, by definition, *has to have a significant chance of failure*. Otherwise, it's just something that someone else has done – it's not innovative.

DON'T FAIL FAST, LEARN FAST

When it comes to setting up new businesses, we'd never start anything if we just listened to the doom-mongers.

Being bombarded with stats like '90% of start-ups fail' or '20% of companies go bust within the first year' isn't exactly encouraging. On the other hand, nowadays, the common refrain in the start-up community tends to be, 'fail fast'. While we should always be aware of survivorship bias – those companies that lived to tell the tale – there are plenty of intriguing examples of this approach working.

In 2006, Joe Gebbia and Brian Chesky launched a new website, which they'd designed to allow locals to rent out their spare beds while large conferences were taking place nearby.

Soon afterwards, they discovered that people found it awkward exchanging money in person, and their new business idea stalled. The two designers quickly began testing online payments, and they immediately saw a spike in new users. That was when Gebbia and Chesky – now Chief Product Officer and Chief Executive of Airbnb – realized they had a viable business model. As well as receiving a 3% service fee from hosts, which covered the costs of online payment processing and funded the operation of the platform, they realized they could also charge between 6 and 12% as service fees from guests.

So, the first iteration of their offering didn't work, but is 'failure' a fair description?

A more accurate representation would be that they 'learned fast', which is also a far better lens through which to view effective innovation more broadly, including in your work/life. A culture of experimentation relies upon acknowledging that you rarely arrive at the perfect answer the first time. However, it also depends on creating a structure that ensures 'failure' is never catastrophic. Successful companies don't go all-in on an idea based on the hunch of one individual, much like you wouldn't invest all your savings without thoughtfully considering the possible downside.

So, if the objective is to learn, how do you design an experiment to optimize for doing it quickly?

TESTING HYPOTHESES

Cast your mind back to when you were 11 or 12 years old and you first walked into a science lab at school.

If you were anything like me, the opportunity to light up the Bunsen burners and set stuff on fire was one of the highlights of the week. In hindsight, this is worrying behaviour, but leaving that aside for a moment, your teacher would not have allowed you anywhere near the equipment before declaring a hypothesis about the experiment – a clear and measurable prediction of what you thought would happen.

The same is true in business – we should design experiments that consistently deliver actionable insights, irrespective of the results.

That means we need to ask the right questions in advance:

- What are your underlying assumptions about the problem you're trying to solve?
- How will these assumptions play out?
- What effects might they have on the business or, for that matter, your work/life?

In the early days of Airbnb, for example, the hypotheses may have looked something like this:

> There's always a shortage of hotel rooms whenever a large conference takes place in the city. By enabling residents the chance to offer their homes and rent out their spare beds, we anticipate that 100 visitors unable to book a hotel will embrace the chance to stay with a local.

When they proved that hypothesis, perhaps they then tested for scalability:

As there's an appetite for the service, if we focus on increasing the total number of listings, we'll see a commensurate rise in bookings.

When this 'failed', they would have to analyse whether the fundamental assumption – the more listings, the more bookings – was wrong or if it was some other factor. Through customer interviews (the customers being both hosts and guests in this case), they identified the problem lay with the awkward payment method, so their next hypothesis could have been:

As people find paying face-to-face uncomfortable, we can remove the friction in the payment process by allowing online credit card payments – this will result in a five-times increase in listings, creating more options for potential guests and increasing the total number of bookings.

While their hypothesis would have been closer to the result, they would have also realized the unexpected upside because of the scale of new bookings and the additional revenue sources.

I'm sure that isn't precisely how Joe and Brian's conversations went down, but you get the gist. The discipline of establishing a hypothesis forces you to think about both the desired outcome and possible reasons for failure – what some people call a 'premortem'. Ensuring that the experiment is measurable ensures you have something against which to judge success – this is incredibly useful when assessing the quality of decision-making, which is notoriously tricky, after the fact.

Remember the lessons from Emily Balcetis and the SPAM lab? Our memories are notoriously unreliable, so make sure you record your predictions in advance.

FOCUS ON WHAT YOU CAN CONTROL

While the hypotheses I outlined above may have been fictional, Airbnb's founding story and their unerring focus on creating a personalized experience for hosts and guests are not, and neither is the flywheel effect that has driven the company's growth:

- Airbnb's favourable terms and easy-to-use technology attracted hosts to the platform, so the increasing number of available properties drew in guests.
- The two-sided review system created a level of trust that encouraged hosts to open up their homes and visitors to book their business trips and holidays in private accommodation rather than hotels.
- As the volume of people using the platform grew, Airbnb invested their rising margins into better tools for hosts and improved search functionality and support for guests.
- All of which led to increasing volumes of data, which is used to further optimize pricing and recommendations, resulting in more listings and more guests – and so on.

One point to consider as you apply these lessons to your work/life is where to focus your efforts.

While you can hypothesize about the likely result of your actions, the nature of experiments is that they don't always work. So, instead of obsessing about the outcome, concentrate on guiding principles and what you can control. In Airbnb's case, their mission is to create a sense of belonging for tourists. If every idea they test has this outcome in mind, positive financial results are much more likely to follow.

- What are your guiding principles?
- How can you test whether you're making progress to achieving this objective?

Amazon is also a proponent of this approach, fundamentally believing that it's only worth testing the parts of the customer experience they can control. As Jeff Bezos said in his April 2010 letter to shareholders:

> Senior leaders that are new to Amazon are often surprised by how little time we spend discussing actual financial results or debating projected financial outputs. To be clear, we take these financial outputs seriously, but we believe that focusing our energy on the controllable inputs to our business is the most

effective way to maximize financial outputs over time. Our goal-setting sessions are lengthy, spirited, and detail-oriented. We have a high bar for the experience our customers deserve and a sense of urgency to improve that experience.

By emphasizing that all experiments are made to improve customer experience and testing *only* inputs under their control, Amazon has created a psychologically safe environment – a vital ingredient for great innovation.

- What can you test that's within *your* control?
- Can you keep your core values and mission in mind whenever you're experimenting?

If you can, rather than beat yourself up when things don't go right the first time, you'll find yourself enjoying how quickly you learn from the results of your tests.

SCRAPPY CAN BE GOOD

None of which means there isn't room for a 'scrappy' or pragmatic approach to how you test new ideas in your work or personal life. After all, you'll never get started if you get stuck at the planning stage.

Even Airbnb still advocates being a 'cereal entrepreneur' in their brand values after a stunt in which they made an impromptu decision to create branded cereal boxes of the Democratic Presidential candidates in 2008. At the time, they were only receiving a couple of bookings a day on the platform, but the cereal unexpectedly sold out. The money raised not only cleared most of their debt; in the process, the story was covered in the national press, and their fortunes turned around.

Starting new projects often depends on doing new things and learning on the job. What's critical is remembering to keep that long-term vision in mind and ensuring your experiments are measurable. The question is then the scale of the test. There are times for taking large, calculated risks like pivoting your company or career, but you only do it when you're basing the decision on an informed judgement.

Otherwise, you should start by making smaller bets and ask yourself these questions:

- What's the itch that you want to scratch?
- Why do you think that it presents an opportunity?
- What's the worst that can happen if it flops?

We're living and working in an ever more complex world, and things are evolving fast. Mistakes will happen, and not every test will go as expected, but a determination to learn quickly will give you the knowledge and inspiration to create bigger and better things.

As Scott Adams, author and creator of the world-famous cartoon strip Dilbert, put it:

> Creativity is allowing yourself to make mistakes. Art is knowing which ones to keep.

Experimentation is a fundamental part of the Work/Life Flywheel and since digital content offers an opportunity to test at scale, let's look at how to design a content flywheel that works for you.

─────── SUMMARY ───────

- Imposter syndrome can breed humility, help you appreciate how others support your ambitions, and spur you on to succeed.
- Innovating requires frequent failure as you push the boundaries of what's possible.
- Learning fast is crucial as you develop a culture of experimentation in your work/life.
- Use testable hypotheses to help you measure the effectiveness of your experiments.
- Instead of obsessing about outcomes, concentrate on guiding principles and what you can control.
- Starting new projects often depends on doing new things and learning on the job, but always keep your 'north star' in mind.
- A determination to learn quickly will give you the knowledge and inspiration to create bigger and better things.

14

The content flywheel

In February 2020, I'd never produced any digital content and never spoken publicly about the future of work.

At the time of writing, I've published over 100 podcasts and newsletters, listened to and read by thousands globally. I now get paid to write articles and share my insights with audiences of industry leaders. Most obviously, I'm writing this book. How have I managed to achieve this career pivot? By following my curiosity and creating a content flywheel.

But why does this matter in the context of the changing future of work?

Because something profound has changed, driven by technology and the internet, in particular. Knowledge was a twentieth-century differentiator. Now everyone can access facts with a Google search, it's no longer about what you know but *how you communicate ideas*.

By the time you finish this chapter, you'll have a reason to do something you don't often do – think in public.

PUBLIC THINKING

I'm willing to guess you've not spent much time sharing your thoughts with the rest of the world. Most of us don't. In this context, when it comes to work, our minds tend to jump to the concept of 'thought leadership' – a horrible phrase suggesting self-importance and pressure to be profound – or 'personal branding' – a problematic idea you read about in Chapter 9.

But even if you felt like you should do these things to help your career, it's more than likely the reason you'd give me for staying silent is a lack of time.

While you're not alone, you're missing a massive opportunity.

Most people never engage in public thinking (which I'm using as shorthand for speaking at conferences or on podcasts, writing thought leadership pieces, posting on social media or in any other public forum). It's easy to justify not doing something if you don't have any positive data to demonstrate its value, so let me break it down for you – done right, it will improve your personal reputation and improve your career prospects. If you're running a business or plan to start one, this habit will increase your chances of winning new business and attract the best people to come and work with you.

REASONS WHY YOU **DON'T** DO IT

Although time is the most common reason for staying silent, it's not the only one.

Here are a few more you might recognize (although one or two may require you to be really honest with yourself):

'I'm afraid of sounding stupid.'
'I don't believe it works.'
'I've got nothing to say.'
'That's not my job.'

The good news is that it's never too late to start. As I well know.

For the decade I ran my digital agency, I did almost everything to avoid putting myself and my opinions out there. I used all the excuses above at some point, but my main issue was a fear of being boring or saying something wrong. If you shoved me onto a stage and forced me to do it, I was fine, but the idea of making public thinking part of my business strategy was at best an indulgence and, at worst, a potential embarrassment.

Fortunately, I've got over myself and learned the power of sharing my ideas both for my personal development and, more importantly, creating value for the businesses and people I work with.

Here's how I dispelled each of those common excuses and why you should too.

REASONS WHY YOU *SHOULD* DO IT

TIME

Sure, I understand. There's never enough time to do everything, and it can often seem more pressing to do the things that create a measurable outcome right there and then. When you live a busy life, you probably weigh up what delivers the maximum value in the time available. But when you say you don't have time to do something, what you really mean is you have other priorities, so here's why you need to bump public thinking up that list.

Thinking in public requires articulating the value you create and doing so will spark new opportunities as you develop a reputation for clear thinking and effective communication.

As billionaire investor Warren Buffett once said:

> If you improve your communication skills, both written and verbal, I guarantee you that you will earn fifty per cent more money over your lifetime. If you can't communicate, it's like winking at a girl in the dark — nothing happens. You can have all the brainpower in the world, but you have to be able to transmit it. And the transmission is communication.[32]

EFFECTIVENESS

The most common objection I hear from people who start sharing their ideas in public is the limited reach of their content.

---

[32] www.linkedin.com/posts/michael-hood-aa2912b0_what-an-honour-to-share-an-evening-with-a-activity-6475070126298406912-9jBQ/

Think again – this is a good thing! When you start publishing online, almost everyone makes the same mistake – being too broad. Don't focus on total numbers of views or clicks, but rather on how many of your specific target audience you meaningfully engage. That means being very clear about who you're talking to and what's important to them.

To build credibility and trust with your audience, concentrate on how you can help answer the questions that they care about in a way they'll remember. If your objective is to hire great talent, for example, there's a clear argument for investing more time in sharing your values and point of view, not least with younger people, who are now entering the workplace with different expectations and priorities. According to a 2021 study by professional services firm, EY, instead of prioritizing money, 63% of Gen Z workers 'feel it is very or extremely important to work for an employer that shares their values'.

Digital platforms allow you to engage individuals at scale, but those people want to hear genuine, well-considered thinking from a real human being. You!

POINT OF VIEW

'But what right do I have to share my ideas? What do I know, and, anyway, hasn't it all been said before?'

We've all been there. Imposter syndrome rears its ugly head in many areas of our work/lives, but no more so than when it comes to public thinking. So, go back to focusing on your niche. Don't try to copy the ideas of others because people quickly see through it.

Think about where your interests and knowledge intersect with the problems your constituency is interested in solving and use them to help tell a story that resonates. What do you know that others don't, which will help you frame those problems differently? Having been nominated for two Pulitzer Prizes and become known as one of the world's leading experts on human performance, Steven Kotler knows a thing or two about public thinking. He shared this nugget with me:

I always tell people, when you're trying to present yourself and your ideas to the world, there are only three things you have: your history, your research and your style.

Your experience and point of view are unique, so share them!

FEAR

Finally, the big one: 'Will I look stupid if this isn't "successful"?'

If we're brutally honest with ourselves, this is the real reason most of us avoid public thinking. The easiest way to get over that fear is to reframe it. Flip it around. Consider how you'll feel if you don't achieve your potential because you didn't give something a try? What have you really got to lose?

Remember the lesson from Daniel Pink's book, *The Power of Regret*:[33] failing to be bold is far riskier in the long run than failing to share your thoughts with the world.

HOW TO GET STARTED

I'm not advocating that you drop all your important tasks to spend all day on LinkedIn and start spouting off about the first thing that comes into your head. Take some time to consider what you're passionate about sharing with others. What is it that you'd love to tell potential clients and collaborators?

Then take these small first steps:

1. Be clear about who you'll be talking to and what they're interested in.
2. Focus on your niche – where do your skills and interests overlap to help you tell a story to your audience? Remember, it's just a starting point, so don't get too hung up on it.

---

[33] Daniel H. Pink, *The Power of Regret: How Looking Backward Moves Us Forward*, Canongate Books, 2022.

3. Start collecting ideas whenever they come to you and jot them down in a notepad or a notetaking app on your phone.
4. Begin adding thoughtful social media comments on topics relevant to your niche.
5. Experiment with sharing something significant that's happened in your workday using different media – you may be more comfortable with audio or video than writing, for example.
6. Don't be scared about offering an informed opinion.
7. Keep going even if there's little engagement initially. It takes time.

The future of work will be increasingly personalized. Our ability to clearly communicate our expertise and perspective to the right people is critical. Start thinking in public today, and you'll soon realize the benefits not just to your confidence to express ideas but to the success of your career. However, to sustain the approach over the long term, you need a couple of things.

1. The intrinsic motivation to keep at it, which is why it should tie in with your Ikigai and niche.
2. A content flywheel to help you capture ideas, synthesize and then communicate them.

Let's dig into that first point.

THE ART OF CURATION

Hung Lee can't tell me *exactly* why he started his newsletter, *Recruiting Brainfood*, but he thinks it was something to do with changes in personal data laws, which is as good a reason as any, I suppose.

Having worked in talent and recruitment throughout his career, he had built up an extensive network and knew that to maintain the value of these relationships, he'd need to obtain their consent to continue contacting them. He asked himself what he could send from the outset that would make them say yes to being on an email list? What value could he share with his audience to allow him to communicate with them whenever he needed to do so?

He started with a simple idea – collecting and sharing the most interesting links he found online each week – it remains the format of *Recruiting Brainfood* to this day.

> These are operational recruiters and HR people. They actually have jobs, and a boss on their case saying, 'do this, do that'. Ultimately, that means they don't have time to freewheel across the internet like I might have, and find all this stuff. So, what I promise to them is that I'll show you maybe ten things this week that you wouldn't have found that may be useful, and will definitely be interesting for your career and what you do.

Five years later, tens of thousands of people every week receive the newsletter in their inboxes every Sunday morning, and Hung is recognized as one of the UK's leading talent experts.

Through curating the ideas of others, he has become a successful public thinker himself, and, as always happens, the success of the newsletter format led to other opportunities.

- He now has a job board, which gives him an insight into trends in the recruitment industry, meaning he's constantly **learning**.
- He has built an active **community** of subscribers who benefit from the content he shares and the ability to easily connect with others who share the same interests.
- He has a platform to **experiment** with new business ideas.

That's not to say it has been an easy process.

As almost all creators experience, it took plenty of time and effort, often with little feedback or recognition, before momentum took over and Hung's investment started paying off. However, once you've nurtured an audience and consistently demonstrate the value you offer them, writing a newsletter can prove lucrative, as proven by other *Future Work/Life* podcast guests like technology writer and

investor Azeem Azhar (*Exponential View*) and the *Category Pirates* –
Christopher Lochhead and Nicolas Cole.

In Hung's case, he monetizes it through sponsorship and adjacent
businesses, but there are times when it can feel like a real slog, which is
why intrinsic motivation matters:

> If you're just jumping on a bandwagon – let's say you think,
> oh, NFTs are the next thing, let's do a newsletter on that
> – it may be good for a while, but you will eventually run
> out of motivation. If you're not genuinely interested in this
> world, the audience will be able to tell. It's something weirdly
> intuitive and artistic, if that makes sense. It's like when you
> sometimes go to a craft beer place, and there's some weird
> dude at the back, and he's totally overly enthusiastic about
> this particular ale or whatever, and you can just tell that this
> guy's well into it. Therefore you trust his angle because he's
> got a depth of knowledge that can only come from a passion
> for the work.

LOOK FOR SIGNALS

Liz Ogabi's family originated in Nigeria, but she'd never lived there
until she got a job at Unilever soon after graduating from university.
Five years later, the entrepreneurial spirit of the people she met
and worked with in Lagos had rubbed off on her and given her the
confidence to pursue her ideas in public.

Having written a little about her experience of business culture
in Nigeria on social media, she found people responding whenever
she posted thoughts about career development, entrepreneurship
and wellbeing for women. Deciding to explore the ideas further, she
contacted writers on LinkedIn who agreed to share content on these
themes for a content website she launched called *For Working Ladies*. As
traffic to the site grew and readers became more engaged, a community
of like-minded people emerged, leading Liz to launch a podcast and
get a publishing deal.

Her book, *Side Hustle in Progress*, was a deep dive into what it takes to get a solo or entrepreneurial career off the ground, but it was also the manifestation of Liz's own side hustle.

She developed a content flywheel by spotting signals in the social media noise – her friends and followers resonating with musings about start-up culture – which gathered momentum and, eventually, allowed her the freedom to quit her day job by monetizing her insights and community.

CREATING A CONTENT FLYWHEEL

Shifting to a creator's mindset doesn't come easy but it can be incredibly rewarding.

The 'a-ha' moment came for me when I realized that two things I enjoyed doing in my spare time – reading and listening to podcasts – were the starting point to reimagine the next step in my career. Once I began, the momentum kept building.

Here's how I got my content flywheel spinning:

- **Listening**: I don't just listen to the same few podcasts on rotation. I introduce new shows on wildly different themes each week to broaden my insights.
- **Reading**: When I hear something I like, I find the speaker's work, online or in their books. Reading remains the fastest way to deepen understanding and knowledge.
- **Recording**: If I'm curious about someone's work, I invite them onto the podcast. Shaping the questions based on my curiosity accelerates my learning and means the guest's experience is unique rather than following the formula of other shows.
- **Writing**: Conversations reveal multiple insights, which feed into my newsletter and now provide a reservoir of ideas for digital and analogue content.
- **Iterating**: Using data to analyse which ideas resonate best helps uncover the themes I should focus on, guiding my discovery of possible new collaborators through more podcast listening.

Continually creating and testing is critical and your curiosity will keep the flywheel turning. But best of all, when you share your thinking in public, people will be drawn to you, creating the opportunity to build your community.

SUMMARY

- It's no longer about what you know but how you communicate ideas.
- Most people never engage in public thinking because of a perceived lack of time, fear of looking stupid or having nothing profound to say.
- Thinking in public demonstrates the value you create, sparks new opportunities, and improves your reputation.
- Consistently addressing your audience's problems builds credibility and trust.
- The future of work will be increasingly personalized, and the ability to communicate your expertise and perspective to the right people is critical.
- Curating the ideas of others can be as valuable as sharing your own.
- Look for signals about what people need help with, through questions and engagement on social media.
- Create a content flywheel based on your interests.
- Share your unique perspective with the world!

Community

Mindset

Breakthroughs

Creativity

WORK/LIFE
FLYWHEEL

Learning

Experimentation

Community

15

Cultivating your network

As work has changed, so has the nature and importance of communities.

It has never been easier to find your 'tribe' online, which creates tremendous opportunities to collaborate with others in new creative ways and accelerate your learning through the experiences of people from different backgrounds. Over the next couple of chapters, we'll explore why maintaining a sense of connection in our work/lives is critical and dig into how cooperation and collaboration will work in the future.

However, to kick this section off, we need to address the elephant in the room. Cultivating a community requires us to build new relationships, which inevitably means you need to start *networking* your arse off.

If you're anything like me, that sentence is one you've dreaded reading!

THE CASE FOR NETWORKING

Rewind a few years…

It wasn't that I never went to networking events. Or even that when I was there, I didn't wander the room keeping my eye out for interesting people to chat with. It's just that I'd rarely ever actually strike up a conversation. I'm telling you this as someone who may, at that same event, have been up on stage making a presentation to hundreds of people or sitting on a panel answering questions from an audience. I just had a mental block when it came to 'working a room', experiencing the Perspiration, Awkwardness, and Introversion of Networking – or PAIN for short.

I say 'had', but during the COVID-19 pandemic, there weren't too many opportunities for face-to-face networking, which came as a great relief!

However, my podcast has become a beautiful illustration of how and why I've fundamentally changed my view of networks since I started my career transition in February 2020. Aware of my shortcomings when building connections, I made a conscious effort to interact with anyone whose work I was interested in. Quickly realizing these conversations were worth capturing, I started the podcast, leading to dozens more new relationships and, ultimately, this book. Evidence that what begins as an exercise in satisfying your curiosity can lead to something much greater.

As we consider the next step in our careers, it's easy to retreat to what and who we know. It might be an industry we've always worked in or a role that we can do with our hands tied behind our back. Critically, you may only seek the counsel of those closest to you, which, while undoubtedly valuable as a source of support, is the wrong strategy for making big changes. Limiting yourself to such a close-knit group can place unnecessary constraints on your future opportunities.

Why?

Sociologist Mark Granovetter is famous for popularizing the concept of 'strong and weak ties',[34] which explains why there is value

---

[34] Mark S. Granovetter, 'The Strength of Weak Ties', *The American Journal of Sociology*, vol. 78, no. 6 (May 1973).

in gaining a broader perspective from a more diverse collection of people. For starters, these types of connections increase the likelihood of finding new job opportunities. And there are multiple ways to approach this, as Professor Janice McGabe's work explains:

- You might adopt the 'sample' approach, with numerous one-to-one friendships, none of whom know each other.
- Even better, you could focus on 'compartmentalizing' your network, reducing the chances of operating in an echo chamber – the downside of a 'tight-knit' network – and mitigating the risk of losing connection with a single link in the chain.
- In practice, this means building relationships with various groups independent of one another, each bringing to the table a different point of view, set of expertise, and extended network of contacts.[35]

Considering it this way sounds transactional, but I'm not suggesting that we opportunistically build relationships only with people who serve specific aims. Instead, as Adam Grant describes in his book, *Give and Take*,[36] the greatest opportunities often result from reciprocity – as much as we should be thinking about what someone can do for us, we should consider what we can do for them.

How can we create value?

Even *framing* the exercise like this can be useful if you're thinking about pivoting your career, as it's almost inevitable that, at times, you'll question whether your skills and experience are transferable. Here's a great chance to remind yourself why you're legendary!

Of course, as with any part of your work/life, there's a trade-off.

While it's critical to cultivate a robust and diverse network, it's also true that deeper relationships, built on trust and understanding, can inspire confidence and action. The challenge is to find the right combination of each. As Erica Young, a specialist in community and

---

[35] Janice M. McCabe, *Connecting in College: How Friendship Networks Matter for Academic and Social Success*, University of Chicago Press, 2016.
[36] Adam Grant, *Give and Take: A Revolutionary Approach to Success*, Weidenfeld & Nicolson, 2013.

networks, shared with me on the *Future Work/Life* podcast, one way to start is mapping our relationships on a piece of paper or using a tool like PowerPoint or Keynote.

- Write down the names of everyone you can remember connecting with over the past two weeks.
- Draw lines between any that know each other.
- Once you sketch your network, you'll get a sense of its size and level of interconnectedness.

You can then begin to answer the question Erica posed:

If I am the sum of the people I spend time with, *who* am I the sum of?

Mapping the people you spend time with can help you uncover insights like who you get new ideas and opportunities from, which groups influence your habits and behaviours, and, importantly, how resilient your support network is. Much as you might scrutinize your personal development – your skills and experience – use the same lens for your relationships.

In my case, my first objective, two years ago, was to open myself up to the idea of meeting new people and sharing ideas. Significantly, I took advantage of the overwhelming shift to digital communication. While online working has shrunk many people's networks and reduced opportunities to develop those weak ties, I've embraced a format that plays to my strengths and significantly reduces the friction of starting those awkward conversations. If I'm curious about a subject and appreciate someone's ideas, I write a concise and thoughtful note to them – easy. More often than not, they respond and, in many cases, are open to chatting about their work and mine.

I've gone a step further and set myself the goal to collate the knowledge and insights I've gained, to share with the *Future Work/ Life* community. In turn, this has led to more people introducing themselves and to me making introductions to others in my growing network.

Cultivating a network and building a community is, it seems, another magical example of the Work/Life Flywheel in motion, and it has long-lasting effects.

THE SUPPORT NETWORK

Remember Allison Baum Gates from Chapter 1? She was one of my first podcast guests and introduced me to the 'flipped workplace' idea. If you recall, she's a venture capitalist now but previously worked for one of the pioneers of digital education, General Assembly. Moving from a start-up to the world of venture capital may seem like a well-trodden path, but there's a significant difference between the role of an operator and an investor, particularly if you're female in a male-dominated industry.

Fortunately, Allison could lean on her network and specifically the community she'd joined, to help her through the difficult early days of a career transition.

Women remain massively underrepresented in venture capital, representing less than 15% of decision-makers in US firms. All Raise is a community designed to support women on their journey through the industry, including cohort-based programs, which match small groups of women to work with each other, and a coach, for a year.

As Allison said:

> When navigating an industry where there are not a lot of people that look like you, building a network of like-minded peers was a powerful force that helped me stay in venture capital instead of leaving it, like so many other women do. The content we learned was helpful, but ultimately it was the connections I made with my peers that made All Raise such an invaluable resource for me and other women.

Formal communities offer one way of supporting you in making big changes in your career but you can often tap into connections you've built in your previous jobs, which is essential if you decide to go it alone as a freelancer or solopreneur.

Sarah Akanbi spent years training as an accountant at KPMG, reassured about the security of a profession that, let's face it, will never outlive its use. However, as she approached her final exams, she finally gave in to the nagging doubts that it wasn't the job she wanted. Never one to shy away from making big decisions, she packed it in and walked away before completing her qualifications, immediately going travelling around Europe to get away and rethink.

After returning to London, she took on some temporary work at a start-up, where she'd ultimately stay for almost a decade.

She gradually took on more responsibility, learning new skills that made a real difference to people in a growing company. She found her groove, excelling at the difficult job of bringing in talented people to fit seamlessly into a business with a unique culture and high expectations. By the time the company had scaled to 400 members of staff based in offices around the world, Sarah had progressed into a senior HR role but still had an urge to do something new. Although she enjoyed being a member of a close-knit team that had shared the unique experience of scaling quickly – including the pressures and rewards that brings – she knew it was the right time to experience a different working environment.

The move went well initially, but after taking a few short hops into different companies and returning from her second maternity leave, her latest employer made Sarah redundant at the end of 2019, just before the pandemic locked us down.

PREPARING YOUR RUNWAY FOR TAKE-OFF

Rather than this presenting a crushing blow, as it could easily have done in the circumstances, Sarah and her partner reviewed their finances and discussed options. With some savings put away from the sale of shares she'd had from those high-growth years at her previous employer and having been financially prudent while on maternity leave, they calculated that she had around six months to consider her options.

As an aside, a six-month savings runway seems to be the magic number for many of the people I've spoken to who've pivoted careers.

Although, when it comes to it, the money often lasts longer than expected as you adjust your lifestyle and outgoings.

At this point in Sarah's story, she turned to the power of her network and recognized how her expertise might be put to good use.

As the workforces of many organizations dispersed for the first time, her knowledge and expertise in people management and culture for distributed teams were in short supply. Knowing she could double down on her experience of managing HR teams through periods of rapid change, and having built so many strong relationships, she was the first call and recommendation for anyone looking for support.

Two years later, steady demand for her time has allowed Sarah to niche down even further into those areas in which she has a real passion.

While she self-deprecatingly observes that her luck might run out at some point, it's evident that her network is happy to reciprocate her eagerness to support others in their careers. A desire to make bold decisions at critical moments and a positive and pragmatic response to events outside her control – like redundancy and a global pandemic – have set her on the path to maximizing her independence and monetizing her in-demand skills.

Of course, these choices also allow her to manage her time how she pleases.

With two young kids to get ready for school and childcare every day, mornings aren't the easiest for Sarah, but working independently has given her complete flexibility. She now has complete freedom to do her work *when* and *where* she wants, and the luxury of making decisions about *who* she wants to work with.

During the challenging pandemic years, Sarah discovered that her network wasn't just a list of old colleagues on LinkedIn, but a closely bound, supportive community.

EVOLVING YOUR NETWORK INTO A COMMUNITY

For Filipe Macedo, cultivating community has always felt like a natural part of his work/life.

After studying computer science, he had a brief career as a DJ, which certainly requires knowing how to engage a crowd. After hanging up his headphones, his creative instincts led him into the advertising industry, and working with clients like Nike and L'Oréal allowed him to indulge his passion for exploring how to use technology to create exciting new experiences. But equally as important was the chance to build relationships with a wide network of like-minded folks.

> Building communities is something I have always tried to do throughout my career, from doing a newsletter to trying to implement a personal CRM to keep up with people.

In 2019, after a decade of working with some of the world's biggest brands, Filipe decided to take a year-long sabbatical.

While the chance to slow down and reflect was one factor, he isn't the type of character to slink off to a beach to drink margaritas and read novels. He had a clear objective to continue his personal development during his year off work, and like any good goal-setter, he knew the best way to achieve this was to hold himself accountable. He decided to involve his network in an experiment, asking them to 'invest' in his sabbatical – essentially crowdfunding his break in return for regular updates about what he was up to and summarizing what he was learning.

You probably think this sounds too good to be true, but, remember, Filipe had been sharing his knowledge and insights with his potential supporters for years.

Having consistently delivered interesting and valuable knowledge to his community, it wasn't far-fetched to imagine they'd buy into his future.

> I was thinking it would be cool to bring the idea of having people investing in my sabbatical. The upside of that would be them getting to know all my experiments and the learnings. So, basically, I would have shareholders in my sabbatical that would buy shares, and I would have to do weekly shareholder reports to make sure I was achieving what I intended to.

Meanwhile, Filipe's old course mate from university, Pedro Oliveira, had also decided to take some time off.

Nearly nine years after founding his online talent platform business, he'd decided it was time to step aside and hand over the reins to a new CEO. After many years of working intensely to scale the business and grow his team, he needed a break. A sabbatical offered Pedro the chance to step back and reflect on everything he'd learned and set some new goals for the next stage of his career.

> It was amazing because you go from this focused mode into a different mode in which you just do things for the sake of learning. I did a course on psychology, and a few other things, including blockchain and Web3, and it all just clicked. A dormant idea I'd had suddenly came back to life and Filipe was one of the first people I talked to.

Reflecting on how critical his network had been in supporting his career and making his last business a success, Pedro envisioned developing a platform which would give undiscovered talent access to backers who could provide financial and mentoring support.

Recognizing how 'tokenomics' – the economic incentives created by using cryptocurrencies and assets – could create new opportunities to invest in individuals, Pedro and Filipe cut short their sabbaticals.

Leaning on their existing networks, they quickly got to work creating a business plan before raising venture capital and hiring a team. Their business, Talent Protocol, is Web3's first professional network and is designed to allow high-potential talent to build their *own* support networks, who can then invest in their futures.

Whether building the right mix of weak and strong ties or transforming loose connections into committed communities, the power of your network will drive your Work/Life Flywheel.

SUMMARY

- Communities have never been more important.
- Finding your tribe creates tremendous collaboration and learning opportunities.
- It's essential to maintain relationships with your 'weak ties' to develop a broader range of opportunities.
- Aspiring for reciprocity helps you identify your value and create inspiring possibilities with others.
- Formal communities provide support and guidance when changing careers or entering new industries.
- Preparing a financial runway gives you options when pivoting your career – many people aim for six months of flexibility.
- Technology facilitates new ways of nurturing relationships and enabling your network to become a committed community of supporters.

16

Connection and collaboration

Among the numerous significant changes to our work/lives over the past few years, the place we spend our time actually *doing the work* has to be the most obvious.

So what are the potential consequences of reducing or completely removing face-to-face interactions? Will this change in behaviour fundamentally change how we relate to one another?

Bruce Daisley is an author and former Vice-President of Twitter. When we spoke on the *Future Work/Life* podcast, he pointed out that while plenty of us would have a sense that we've become more efficient since our shift to remote work, few would profess to have experienced more joy. To illustrate why this might be the case, he gives the fantastic example of the idea of *Simcha*, a Hebrew word, which, although literally translated as joy, is only experienced collectively.

Has a lack of relatedness to one another, caused by the lack of a shared physical experience, removed the opportunity for *Simcha* at work?

Certainly, when I cast my mind back to working in the office, I remember many random moments of laughter and relationships built through shared experiences, both positive and challenging. Could I honestly tell you my life working remotely is full of these emotions? No, but then I guess the point here is what's the trade-off we're willing to accept? Is it more important for me to get my fill of *Simcha* in the office or work close to my family, exercise bike and a comfortable spot to nap?

Well, this needn't be a binary choice – either fully remote or office-based – and there are other ways we can create connections with people.

For example, among well-established, fully distributed teams, regular meet-ups are an essential part of the culture. However, rather than focus on meeting every week, they may congregate monthly or quarterly instead. Regular off-site events can offer the best of both worlds – the opportunity for longer-term strategic conversations with some good old bonding sessions.

But if you're thinking about 'going it alone', how can you cultivate that all-important *Simcha*?

Well, thank goodness for the internet.

ANALOGUE AND DIGITAL CONNECTIONS

Developing new relationships with a diverse collection of collaborators is now easier than ever. If you decide to go it alone, as a freelancer, solopreneur or by starting a business, there are plenty of accessible, exciting ways to build connections:

- You can replicate a team environment with the people you work alongside in flexible working spaces (just without shared clients and colleagues).
- You can arrange regular interactions with a select group of industry colleagues or a mastermind group.
- You can even join online communities and take the relationships off-line to meet in person – I've enjoyed doing this several times as part of cohort-based courses over the past couple of years.

Talking of cohort-based courses, these offer one of the most effective ways to build your community.

There are increasing numbers of digital courses that focus on every conceivable topic and area of interest. The best of them combine the key characteristics that feed your flywheel – open-mindedness and the pursuit of a specific goal, the ability to come up with and test new creative ideas, and the opportunity to learn alongside others. The advantage of cohort-based courses over those available on-demand is that they introduce all-important accountability into the process. When you work through a program as a group, you're more likely to put into practice what you've learned, than if you're studying alone.

Courses are a great opportunity to learn from others, but they can also provide a launchpad to monetize your expertise too.

A natural evolution of building digital products and expertise from working with clients in your niche, is designing a course. You might start with an on-demand offering, which people can access whenever they wish, providing you with passive income via a product that lives forever. Or, by developing your own cohort-based course, you can combine getting paid to share your insights with the possibility to grow a community around your ideas.

Whatever the scenario, although the location and frequency with which we congregate with others will change, it's both possible and desirable to cultivate relationships that offer genuine connection and a sense of relatedness that we can otherwise miss when working in isolation.

MAXIMIZING THE VALUE OF GROUP EXPERIENCES

While there are occasions for relaxed social meet-ups and casual conversations, as group interactions become less frequent, it's worth considering how to maximize the value of collaborative sessions. If you want to do this successfully, you need to create the following conditions:

- **Shared goals**: Make sure everyone understands and is aligned with the session's objectives.
- **The right level of complexity**: The challenge should be significant enough to engage everyone's full attention but not so complicated that achieving it is impossible in the time available.

- **Full attention**: Solving the problem requires everyone's attention – no taking a call mid-meeting and certainly no responding to emails.

- **Equal participation**: Not only should everyone's voice be heard, but the whole group should share a common language, meaning you need a relatively level playing field when it comes to subject matter expertise.

- **Open communication and close listening**: You need to listen carefully to what everyone is saying. Collaboration is an opportunity to create new perspectives, not reinforce opinions.

- **'Yes culture'**: Constructive disagreement and divergent opinions are a natural and essential part of business, but in a collaborative session, it's far more effective to build on someone's point, not shoot it down.

- **Novelty and unpredictability**: There are few things worse than when you feel like you're constantly covering the same ground. Ensuring that ideas are always progressing and introducing something unexpected can force everyone to pay close attention.

- **Blending egos and deep embodiment**: The best collaborative sessions require us to leave our egos at the door. If the group trusts one another to find the best solution collectively, you create the potential for magic to emerge.

- **Control**: We should aim for the right balance of openness to others' opinions while maintaining the confidence that we can express our own.

If you're eagle-eyed, you might have spotted that these are the group flow triggers I promised to share with you in Chapter 10.

Like our experience of individual flow, the more we dial up each of the triggers, the deeper into flow we'll go. As a reminder, flow increases **productivity** by 500%, amplifies **creativity** by between 400% and 700% and improves **learning** rates by 490%, and these effects show up most frequently in our interactions with others. Complete concentration and focus are prerequisites for flow and characterize the moments of connection with others, whatever the mode of communication.

Rather than see digital interactions as barriers to building connections, contemplate the opportunities they present instead. Not least how cooperating in exciting ways opens up our eyes to radically new ideas for monetizing our experience and interests.

THE COOPERATION ECONOMY

As work becomes more personalized and increasingly specialized, the nature of jobs will change too.

Being able to slot in to a new team to solve very specific problems will become a prerequisite for those most in-demand, which means developing our 'soft' skills. Many of these skills relate to how we communicate and collaborate with others, including an ability to quickly adapt and get up to speed on the priorities of a project, something the best freelancers and consultants master.

The evolution of this idea will be what writer and venture capitalist Packy McCormick calls 'Liquid Super Teams'[37] – groups of people who come together to leverage their highly specialized sets of skills. These groups of people will not be bound by location or even time zone but will combine because their expertise and philosophy complement one another. Packy McCormick describes how these teams represent the idea of a new 'cooperation economy', which will create new possibilities for your career by supercharging:

> The benefits of building something for yourself by creating networks of individuals who are able to enhance each other's capabilities, while retaining the power of the Person. They're the good parts of a company and going solo, rolled into one.

In this new arrangement, since the commitment required from each individual is low, you attract a broader set of talented people. At the same time, you remove the costs of a traditional organization, creating

---

[37] www.notboring.co/p/the-cooperation-economy-#:~:text=That's%20a%20Liquid%20Super%20Team,optionality%2C%20and%20everyone%20has%20upside

more value for customers. Also, since groups of freelancers and solopreneurs will have their own audience and proven systems, the liquid structure benefits from an expanded network and community.

There's another advantage from pooling expertise globally, rather than in close proximity – you increase the chances of cognitive diversity.

People's background, upbringing, education and interests all play a part in how they think. Their lived experience contributes to their outlook, beliefs and how they approach subjects like problem-solving and creativity. All of which is why it makes career and business sense to prioritize creating a diverse and inclusive team. Companies can learn something from this, too, as Tamika Curry Smith, Nike's former Vice-President of Diversity & Inclusion, explained on the podcast. In particular, the importance of communicating clearly that putting together diverse teams is an objective, even if you haven't cracked it yet. As she observed, 'progress doesn't mean perfection', but as with any positive change, you've got to start somewhere.

What differentiates any great team is that it comes together to be greater than the sum of its parts. While 'liquid super teams' aren't commonplace (yet!), the principle of pulling together teams of flexible experts *is* already working.

THE EVOLUTION OF TEAMS

After Stephanie Nadi Olson returned to work following the birth of her second daughter, she quickly realized she was back too soon.

As a successful advertising executive, she'd always been someone in a hurry. Still, after experiencing postpartum depression, she reflects on how she should have eased back into her high-pressure sales role more slowly. Even better would have been to redesign how she worked – perhaps partly in-person and partly remote. But this was 2015 when no one had even heard the expression hybrid work, and a request to do a couple of days at home was an admission that you didn't take your job seriously.

Oh, how things have changed.

A year after her maternity leave ended and having to suck up working with a 'nightmare boss', she had the 'kick up the butt' she needed. She sat down with her husband, looked at their finances, and determined she had six months to figure out if the idea she'd had brewing was viable.

What was the business?

She was making a bet that she wasn't the only one who needed more flexibility and independence in their work. Jump forward to 2022, and it's fair to say she nailed that one:

> People were saying, gosh, can I do a job share, can I go down on the number of hours that I work after I have a baby? Can I work remotely because I'm caring for a sick parent? And across the board in marketing, almost unequivocally, they were being told: no. They're being told it's impossible. And then COVID lifted the veil. All of the stuff that we'd been told was bullshit.

Stephanie's business, We Are Rosie, was perfectly positioned to take advantage of several converging trends – increasing burnout among in-house marketing teams, higher demand for flexibility in the workforce, and advancements in technology allowing improved synchronous and asynchronous collaboration. Although we're seeing a trend towards people going solo, We Are Rosie is an example that we still want to come together to achieve great things, but now we also want the freedom to choose *when* and with *whom* we do it. After all, if you look at the data on engagement and satisfaction in the workplace, people will typically cite working in a team as the most fulfilling part of the job.

One of the beauties of controlling your pattern of work and having agency over which clients you work with is that you can gradually shape your work/life to your own desire. This is why more and more independent workers – whether small business owners, freelancers or contractors – are coming together in formal or informal collectives – whether in a liquid super team or through platforms like We Are Rosie. They create the communities we need in the absence of a full-time employer. And that matters.

As Stephanie told me:

> We all learn from each other, and we try to be really open about how we're feeling and how things are going, because honestly, building a business this quickly is no joke. We have been in the trenches together. We have been through some shit. We have done really hard things. We have cried on each other's shoulders. We have celebrated incredible victories. And we have that sense of community.

Very soon into We Are Rosie's journey, Stephanie recognized that however diverse the teams that were collaborating on client projects – in terms of location, background and skillset – they all shared a common goal – a mission to show the world that the model could work. They all had an incentive to demonstrate that this new way of working was sustainable and effective for clients, knowing that validating this allowed them to continue designing their perfect work/life – one which combined flexibility, ambition, and security.

> They wanted to be able to do that forever because they love the autonomy and freedom and the creativity... but their fear was 'I'm not going to have the next client, and then I'm going to have to go take a regular job. And I really don't want to, but if I can't fill my client pipeline, that's going to be the end result.' So, We Are Rosie shows up on the scene and says, we want to prove to the world that this way of working makes sense. And we want to fill your pipeline for you so that you can work in a way that makes sense for your life.

Leaping into solo and entrepreneurial life can seem scary, but communities can provide a bridge to the freedom and opportunities you're searching for. Joining an existing community can be a great way to build your confidence and get you started. The projects may provide a valuable additional revenue stream to grow your business. Or, as in the case of one 'Rosie' (as platform users are known), taking on some work allowed her to build the specific skills and knowledge to raise venture capital investment for her digital marketplace.

However you choose to nurture your community, you'll find it brings you the chance to experiment and build new connections, and provides an incredible opportunity to keep learning.

SUMMARY

- The risk of remote work is less connectedness with others.
- Businesses need to reimagine how in-person interactions can enable more collaboration and build trust and connection between people.
- The internet now allows you to develop new types of relationships with people around the world.
- Cohort-based courses combine learning, collaboration, networking and accountability.
- They also present a fantastic opportunity for you to monetize your expertise.
- Thinking intentionally about how to design collaboration sessions allows you to maximize the value of 'group flow'.
- Liquid super teams are examples of how cognitively diverse people can come together to leverage their highly specialized sets of skills, unbound by location or time zone.
- While we're seeing more people go it alone, new technology and communities provide the tools to work collaboratively on projects.

Learning

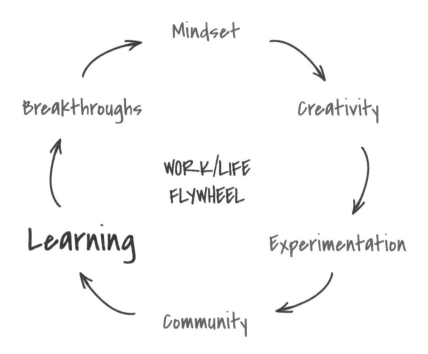

Mindset

Creativity

Breakthroughs

WORK/LIFE
FLYWHEEL

Experimentation

Learning

Community

17

Lifelong learning

It's the 21st of August 2004 on Lake Schinias, and the final of the 2,000m coxless pairs rowing at the Athens Olympics is nearing its conclusion.

As the British duo, Cath Bishop and Katherine Grainger, pull their final few strokes and cross the finish line, they both know they've just raced at their absolute peak. Struggling to breathe and unable to see clearly, they can't tell for sure where they've finished, but after years of dedication and sacrifice, know they couldn't have done any more. They're directed towards the medal presentation area and discover they've won silver. Finally, they can celebrate their achievement.

Yet, in sport, success is so often judged based on who finishes *first*, and Cath Bishop already has conflicting thoughts going through her mind while receiving her well-earned medal. These thoughts and questions about what winning and success mean, stay with her, eventually leading her to write *The Long Win*[38] in 2020.

> We had done everything we could, we had made the podium, we had come second. How should I make sense of that?

---

[38] Cath Bishop, *The Long Win: The Search for a Better Way to Succeed*, Practical Inspiration Publishing, 2020.

REFRAMING SUCCESS

The careers of elite sportspeople are often measured in wins, losses and draws – clear metrics that make it easy for us to judge whether they were 'successful' or not. Although, of course, without context, this tells us very little, not least how the individuals themselves judge success.

As Cath writes:

> The separation of 'performance' and 'results' is becoming second nature to most elite athletes. It doesn't mean that results aren't important, far from it, but it recognises that an athlete can develop. Results can never be guaranteed or controlled. They depend on external factors, ranging from conditions to the weather, referees and umpires, not to mention your competitors. I know first-hand that it's a completely different experience to sit on the start-line of a race waiting to deliver your best performance than to sit there feeling that you have to win. Those two experiences are worlds apart, and the performances that follow usually are too.

Following what, by any measure, was a highly successful sporting life, but one that was, as a result of the inevitable ups and downs of competition, punctuated by periods of self-doubt and self-criticism, Cath began reframing her view on winning. She observed that our obsession with winning – whether in sport, business or life – holds us back and that we need new ways of measuring success.

Take education, for example.

Sir Ken Robinson's TED talk, 'Do Schools Kill Creativity?', is the most-watched of all time. Yet, despite his articulation of why we need to shake education up, we still seem to be sticking with methods of teaching and measurement of performance that make little allowance either for the individual characteristics of our children, or the necessity that we prepare them for an uncertain and rapidly evolving future.

The same is true in our work/lives, in which it's all too tempting to measure your success against that of your peers.

I've been guilty of this in the past, and social media hasn't helped. Whether it's virtue signalling on Twitter, humble bragging on LinkedIn or sharing filtered photos of the perfect life on Instagram, focusing on the 'achievements' of others is a thankless task. Of course, when you dig below the surface, things are often not what they appear in other people's lives, so you should focus your energy on creating a work/ life that gives *you* purpose and in which *you* feel like you're making progress.

And anyway, what's the big hurry? We're all going to be living and working for a lot longer, so we're better off settling in for the long haul!

THE MULTI-STAGE LIFE

Lynda Gratton and her colleague, Andrew Scott, have examined how life expectancy changes the way we learn, work and rest. They identified a fundamental shift in how we think about our lives, as we've moved on from a traditional three-stage life – full-time education, followed by full-time work, and finally, full-time retirement – to a multi-stage life.

The idea of the average person working for 40 years and then retiring to a quiet life is behind us. Instead, advances in technology and the rapidly changing demands of the labour market will require us to be constantly reskilling and adapting. A longer, healthier life will require – or I prefer to think of it as *allow* – people to work until much later. However, rather than being condemned to non-stop work, these years will be scattered with sabbaticals and periods of more intense education.

The university of life will truly last a lifetime.

A longer life will also lead to more people starting their own businesses, developing portfolio careers as they master new skills, and developing broader networks. Whereas in the past, our paths may have closely followed others in our age cohort, consistently starting new pursuits such as courses and entrepreneurial ventures will expose us to more diverse collaborators. This is what Lynda is finding. She's a 67-year-old who spends much of her time chatting with other entrepreneurs in their twenties and thirties because they're experiencing the same types of daily challenges and have similar ambitions for their small businesses.

I find this prospect exciting, as does my fellow optimist, Lynda, which is lucky as optimists tend to live longer, healthier lives!

ONGOING LEARNING

While researching this book, I lost count of how many people told me that one of their values is lifelong learning, which is both a contributor to and outcome of building momentum in your Work/Life Flywheel. It is the fuel that continuously powers the engine of your personal growth and the grease that unlocks resulting breakthroughs.

When we talk about learning, our first instinct is to think about formal education, but the truth is we've already learned four of the main lessons that will serve us well as they form the individual parts of our Work/Life Flywheel.

- Stay open-minded to new opportunities and focus your time on learning about things that align with your values and purpose.
- Take a creative approach to leading your work/life, using flow to maximize the rate at which you learn, and understand how stories create connections between people.
- Experiment with new ideas, and don't be afraid to make mistakes, as these often lead to the biggest changes.
- Constantly push yourself to meet new people with different perspectives and backgrounds who'll teach you about new topics and ways of thinking.

With the rate of change happening around us, learning and development must be one of our most significant priorities over the next decade.

At every level of education and work, the type of information we prioritize, and how we teach, will determine how well we respond to societal, environmental and technological challenges. A one-size-fits-all approach is not the way to achieve the results we need. Just as elite sportspeople expect a highly personalized approach to their training and coaching, we must do the same.

The good news is that you've managed the first part by reading this book!

The Work/Life Flywheel provides a model to help you achieve and exceed your potential. Your focus should be on the small actions you can take each day, that compound over time. Flow state's challenge/skills balance is a helpful framework to use as a guide here. By making the challenge 4% harder than your current skill level, you'll hit the sweet spot and get into flow. Try taking this idea into your everyday life.

Constantly aim to be pushing yourself 4% harder each day and before you know it, you'll experience the benefits of compound growth in your career.

SYSTEMS AND THE IMPORTANCE OF TEACHING YOURSELF

Let's be clear, there's another crucial skill you need to develop to thrive in the future of work – the ability and desire to teach *yourself*.

Yes, there's huge value in formal education and structured courses, whether that's for personal or career development. There's also much to be learned from building a community, engaging with experts, and building relationships with people who have varying experiences and divergent perspectives. There comes a point, though, when the difference between ordinary and legendary is what *you* do.

And there's a (long) word for the process of doing this: *autodidacticism*.

To be autodidactic means mastering a subject without the guidance of a teacher and represents the most significant opportunity to differentiate yourself from others, as you:

- Determine the subjects you're most interested in learning about.
- Decide on the depth to which you'll dig to discover more.
- Choose how much time to spend doing it and when.

All of this is within *your* control.

Justin Welsh's experience typifies how your career can take you in new and exciting directions when viewed through this lens. In 2019, after more than a decade working for fast-growth tech businesses, he burned out. Realizing that he needed to make significant changes in his work/life, Justin decided to walk away from his highly paid job and go it alone. But before quitting, he had to build a new revenue stream.

Justin hypothesized that creating attention for himself online represented the greatest possibility for him to develop an independent future as a solopreneur, so he designed a system to help him achieve this.

Three years later, his systems have unlocked new levels of autonomy and financial freedom through constant learning and iteration. He has built a diversified portfolio of one-person internet businesses, several selling the lessons of how people can develop and deploy systems of their own. Nobody showed Justin how to do this. He worked it out for himself by:

- Making an informed decision about how and where to spend his time most effectively (*the hypothesis*).
- Learning the skills to be able to powerfully and succinctly communicate his ideas (*through copywriting*).
- Applying the principles of public thinking to market his new businesses (*sharing his point of view*).
- Being relentlessly clear about where he was going but flexible about how he got there (*consistency*).

Justin's approach is the perfect example of a Work/Life Flywheel, which, as time progresses, builds more and more momentum.

He is laser-focused on his goal of scaling his businesses to $5 million in revenue as a 'diversified entrepreneur', channelling his creativity and drawing on his own experiences to share how his audience (and potential customers) can join him in becoming successful solopreneurs. Justin is constantly experimenting, which he can do at scale using his online community. The insights he gathers feed back into his decisions about product development. None of which would be possible if he didn't carve out time to step back and reflect, which he does by going on long walks with his wife and ensuring he spends time away from the computer with friends and loved ones between Fridays and Sundays.

By combining autodidacticism with well-thought-out systems, Justin has redesigned a more sustainable and rewarding work/life, all while making a difference to hundreds of thousands of others who want to achieve the same.

> What is most likely to allow me to be creative on a regular basis? To keep me writing, to keep me producing, to keep me building, to keep me tinkering. To me, that is systems. Systems are there when motivation or creativity falters. And it will, one day. Systems help you work through that because they tell you, step-by-step, how to turn something into something else.

Incremental improvements, made consistently, add up to life-changing results.

NECESSITY IS THE MOTHER OF INVENTION

I can't tell you how many hours I've spent in front of whiteboards sketching out business models. Depending on your preferred framework, you'll typically try to define your target audience, the channels through which you'll reach them, and key partners and resources. Most importantly, you'll look to clearly articulate your *value proposition* – how your product or service creates value for customers. The value proposition is why a customer will turn to *you* rather than a competitor, which rests on how well you solve *their* problem.

Of course, there are occasions where you're the *only* one solving that problem.

How do you become this rare case? Usually because you're experiencing it acutely *yourself.*

What started as a well-trodden path to a career in finance deviated when Kathrin Hamm's university developed a partnership with a new school in Afghanistan. After volunteering to work on the initiative, she discovered something that had been lacking in her corporate life – purpose. Approaching the end of her studies, she took what most of her peers regarded as a peculiar decision – to move to Afghanistan to work for the school.

She loved it.

Seeing the impact she was making gave Kathrin the incentive to continue her studies, focusing on international development. She studied for a PhD, leading to a prestigious job at the World Bank. What followed were several years of fulfilling work, taking her to every corner of the globe.

And yet, a couple of years later, Kathrin quit her job and founded a start-up selling blankets.

If you'd spent years attaining a PhD, got yourself a great job at a world-renowned organization, making a real difference to people's lives, what would lead you to take such a risk? It's hard to imagine but, of course, we only see life's opportunities through our own eyes. In Kathrin's case, her eyes had become increasingly bleary because the more time she spent away, the less she was able to sleep.

Struggling with chronic insomnia, she tried out every sleep aid on the market, eventually leading her to weighted blankets.

> It's not a new concept. It's been around for thirty years. Even though it was a product that was originally developed for children with sensory disorders, the same mechanisms apply to calming adults and helping them sleep. So I bought one in a German pharmacy. It took six weeks to ship and when it arrived, it looked really ugly. At first, I didn't want to try it but I said let's give it a shot. I slept like never before. So at this point, I was like – this is magic!

The problem was that these were medical blankets and they were filled with 20 pounds of plastic beads, which meant they tended to get hot, so Kathrin found them unusable all year round.

But the seed was sown and her company, Bearaby, was born.

In one of the clearest cases of 'necessity is the mother of invention' that I've come across, Kathrin decided that *she* was the person to create a new category of product. Giving herself a 12-month deadline to see if she could make it work, she set about trying to produce a natural weighted blanket that was both practical and something you'd be proud to share in public.

COMMUNITY RECIPROCITY

Fast forward four years, Kathrin and her team have built a thriving business, which is now selling the Bearaby blanket in major retailers across the United States.

While she explained to me she'd never intentionally sought to become an entrepreneur, it has allowed her the most incredible opportunity she could imagine to follow through on her guiding principle – to be constantly learning.

Switching from being an international development economist to a start-up founder certainly put her outside her comfort zone, but she enjoys throwing herself in the deep end. She even sent cold outreach messages to her peers in a new industry in which she had neither an existing network nor expertise. Fortunately, she discovered a community open to welcoming her into the fold and supporting her development. In the same spirit, she now gives back to her extended network, encouraging others with their entrepreneurial endeavours:

> Having peers at different stages and a community that supports you is really critical early on, and building these relationships is also just really fulfilling as you all grow together. It's really fun.

When it comes to how she designs her work/life, flexibility and opportunities to switch off and reflect are critical. Most impressively of all, she's completely on brand, incorporating a nap into every working day – presumably draped in her tasteful weighted blanket.

SUMMARY

- An obsession with winning will hold you back, so it's essential to reframe success.

- Rather than comparing yourself to others, focus your energy on creating a work/life that gives you purpose and in which you feel like you're making progress.

- A longer, multi-stage life means more people will start their own businesses, develop portfolio careers and develop broader networks.

- As well as formal training, staying open-minded to new experiences and discovering new perspective accelerates your learning.

- Think about your approach to learning in the same way elite sportspeople do about training and coaching – it should be highly personalized.

- Become autodidactic and use systems to keep you on track even when creativity or motivation falters.

- Keep your eyes open for new business opportunities based on problems you experience – how could you help solve them for others?

- Take advantage of communities to help your development and then pay it back to people earlier in their journey.

18

Following your curiosity

A t any stage of our work/lives, we can experience a crisis of confidence and a lack of clarity about what to do next.

For many of the people I've surveyed and interviewed for this book, the further down a particular career path they've travelled, the harder it can be to take a step back and get perspective on what matters. It can feel impossible to work out what to do next after being buried deep into a particular field of work or having established a reputation and expertise in one industry. Even figuring out where your real interests lie can seem like a puzzle. I know this is the case for some parents I've spoken to, who feel like all they do is switch between job mode and child-caring mode. It can be challenging to remember who you really are.

If you're still feeling unclear about any of this, despite having read up to this point, don't worry, I've got a reframe that will help unblock things. So grab a pen and some paper and write down whatever comes into your head.

- Without overthinking it, write down how you spend your time when you have ten minutes to spare.
- When you're not thinking directly about your job, what are you doing?
- If you have an hour to yourself, what do you look forward to?

▪ Picture a week away from your current job. What sort of activities would you enjoy?

For example, if you enjoy podcasts, you might note down what topics you prefer and what style – e.g., interviews, documentaries, analysis. In my case, I listen to various genres and subjects – football, cycling, music, history, entrepreneurship, technology, creativity. I turn to these, not because I feel like I *should* be listening to them but because I enjoy them.

If you wrote down that you'd spend most of your time reading, what books would you choose? Would that differ if you had a week free rather than just an hour? If you delve into non-fiction, what kinds of subjects are you drawn to?

A few more questions, and then we'll move on.

▪ Think for a moment what engaged you while chatting at a party or over dinner? What were you talking about?
▪ If I was to ask your best friend or partner what you love to learn about, what would they say?
▪ What interests do you feel like you haven't had time for over the past five years but would love to dig into again?

As you might expect, this book has been on my mind a fair bit of late, and whenever anybody asks me questions about it, I've found myself repeatedly discussing how much I've loved meeting new people as part of the research. If you've had a conversation with me at any point over the past few months, I'd have told you how much I've enjoyed asking questions about people's stories, exploring why they made the choices they made and what lessons they've learned from them.

I've spent my time learning more about topics I'm interested in, helping people articulate their stories, and then sharing what we've discovered together in my podcast, digital writing, and this book. Yet, when I initially went through my Ikigai in 2020, I'd never have thought that by 2022 I'd produce a podcast and be writing a book. I got here by following my curiosity.

As Dorie Clark shared in her book, *The Long Game:*[39]

> Wherever we are in our lives, we may not yet have identified something overtly meaningful that we want to do or are good at. But we all have things we're interested in and want to learn more about. A passion for photographing birds, for instance, may not seem particularly 'meaningful'. But if it's *interesting*, that curiosity spurs us toward mastery and ultimately may lead in useful directions, such as new personal and professional connections, a book deal, or a successful campaign to preserve local wetlands.

We get so bogged down with the significance of 'discovering our purpose' that it puts us off even starting. Remember, don't overcomplicate it. Concentrate on things that you enjoy and make you feel good.

Here are two ideas to get you started.

1. TRACK YOUR DAILY HIGHLIGHTS

You'll already be doing things that you enjoy, but can you remember them? Every evening, write down a couple of daily highlights. You start noticing patterns when you've been doing this for a while. It could be that you love writing, jamming with people over a campaign idea, or analysing data. Whatever it is, do more of it.

2. NOTICE HOW YOU SPEND YOUR TIME

What do you do for pure enjoyment? It might seem outlandish to incorporate a personal interest into your work, but try introducing it slowly. Perhaps your love of history will bring a different perspective to a client's problem. If you can't get enough of listening to podcasts, could you use them to create a new way of sharing knowledge within your team? The future of work is becoming more personalized, so bring your unique point of view to the party.

---

[39] Dorie Clark, *The Long Game: How to Be a Long-Term Thinker in a Short-Term World*, Harvard Business Review Press, 2021.

WHY CURIOSITY?

You'll remember that when I began redesigning my work/life, I focused on identifying my five guiding principles – the values that would help me decide how to prioritize my time and measure my progress. As a reminder, here they are again:

- Autonomy
- Creativity
- Curiosity
- Growth
- Humour

Among the many smart and successful people I've interviewed in my research, *curiosity* is one of the most recognizable characteristics. Some specifically reference it. Others implicitly display it in how they discuss their interests and passion for work. It's often a value that motivates them to persist even when the going gets tough.

Why is curiosity so valuable?

Tim Harford is a journalist, author of multiple bestselling books, a TV host and the presenter of the chart-topping podcast, *Cautionary Tales*. You probably know him best as The Undercover Economist (after the title of his first book and long-running *Financial Times* column). If you do, you'll understand why I considered him the right person to ask about the importance of curiosity in your work/life. Tim spends much of his time looking for intriguing stories, which offer a fresh perspective on historical and current events. Guided by curiosity and an ability to join dots between seemingly unrelated ideas in new ways, he can simultaneously entertain and inform readers and listeners.

Borrowing the metaphor of the 'Scout Mindset' from Julia Galef,[40] Tim explained that as opposed to many situations in life where you're defending your viewpoint against attack (a 'Soldier Mindset'), curiosity allows you the opportunity to focus on thinking and talking about the *ideas*:

Let's see what's out there. Let's map the terrain.

---

[40] Julia Galef, *The Scout Mindset: Why Some People See Things Clearly and Others Don't*, Portfolio, 2021.

What's more, it implies humility:

> Psychologists talk about the information deficit view of curiosity, which is that it's this kind of itch because you realize there's something you don't know, and you want to figure it out. If you've got no idea what you don't know, you're *not* curious, and if you think you know everything, you're *not* curious. But if you know something and you also know that there are these gaps, that's when you get *very* curious. So that's the reason I say it implies humility because packaged together automatically with curiosity is an acknowledgement there's something I don't know and that I want to know.

Curiosity is, by definition, an ambition to learn and discover more about yourself and the world around you. It's a value worth prioritizing for a lifetime.

GO BACK TO BASICS

As the title of Dorie Clark's book alludes to, not only can applying too short-term a lens to the way we judge success be unhelpful, it misunderstands the timelines required to make real change.

In her work with coaching clients, Dorie sees the same pattern repeating itself over and over. It can take two to three years of consistently sharing ideas publicly before it yields *any* results. This requires incredible patience, but it also emphasizes why it's important to constantly re-evaluate your purpose and goals and ensure that you're getting some enjoyment from the process.

A multi-stage life means we'll have more than one career. While factors outside our control drive some changes in work, we are in charge of how we respond to them. In these moments, it also pays to be aware of what interests us, so we can spot new ways of channelling our curiosity.

Take Jeff Kofman, for example.

Jeff had a 30-year career in the public eye. He gained a reputation as one of the world's leading war correspondents and won accolades, including an Emmy for his coverage of the Libyan Revolution and the downfall of Gaddafi. When he decided to pack journalism in, you might think he'd consider it was time to retire in glory. Or at least step back and take things easy for a while.

For Jeff, the reality wasn't so clear-cut.

In the supposed twilight of their careers, the typical route for reporters is a move into corporate communications or a teaching role. While he was passionate about passing on some of the knowledge he'd accumulated over those years, he didn't envisage permanently settling into that role. After travelling the world reporting on stories as varied as the Chilean miners' rescue – where he was the first international journalist on the scene – the ecological future of the Galapagos Islands and multiple war zones, Jeff wasn't ready to stop sharing stories.

Instead, his career took an unexpected turn. How? Because he kept his eyes open to new possibilities and followed his curiosity.

STORYTELLING AND EXPERIMENTATION

In late 2013, Jeff tagged along with a colleague to a media hackathon in London. After touring the venue chatting in fascination with many of the people involved – 'If I'd met a programmer before that day, I wasn't aware of it' – he was introduced to a team that had developed a solution to align text with audio. A bit like karaoke, you could follow the spoken word and read it at the same time. Since this was a technological world about which Jeff knew absolutely nothing, he asked them a question related to one of the biggest headaches he'd experienced throughout his journalistic career – transcribing interviews.

'Would this work if you used automated speech-to-text to transcribe it?' he asked one of the programmers, 'and make the spoken word searchable?'

Following a short pause, the developer replied, 'It's an interesting idea. We could try.'

At this point, Jeff's second career as an accidental entrepreneur began.

When I say transcribing interviews was a headache for reporters, I'm massively underplaying the sheer waste of talent involved in creating an accurate text copy of interviews. The transcription process invariably requires several highly paid members of the production team and the journalist locking themselves away for days in what Jeff called 'transcription black holes'. Not the best use of time, in other words. A product that could solve this problem was therefore a big deal for thousands of media organizations.

But what did Jeff know about setting up and running a business, let alone building a sophisticated technology product? Absolutely nothing.

Fortunately, he didn't let that stop him. Eight years later, having raised millions of dollars in venture capital and secured investment from *The New York Times* and the Associated Press, Jeff Kofman now leads a fast-growing business. For all that Jeff didn't know about entrepreneurship, he knew about storytelling and, in particular, why solving this problem was a tale that people in his former role would want to hear.

Which isn't to say the process has been easy.

As he put together the business plan for his company, Trint (a word he invented by combining the words 'transcription' and 'interview'), his lack of skills was obvious, and he felt well out of his depth. He'd never managed anyone, could barely use a spreadsheet and, when it came to pitching, had no idea about how to speak the lingo.

Rather than let any of this deter him, he focused on the lessons he'd learned from his career as a reporter. He never bluffed and he used his interviewing skills to ask questions that might have been obvious to other people but which, to him, served as a crash course in business and entrepreneurship. He didn't let his lack of start-up experience get in the way – he embraced it.

I really recommend shaking up life even if you love what you're doing. Shaking up life and getting out of your comfort zone professionally keeps your edge and allows you to avoid coasting into old age and being in a set routine. You're constantly growing. I've learned so much about business, technology, software, innovation, marketing and sales and building a high-performance team. I didn't know anything about these things. There's so much, and there continues to be as the company grows and we face different challenges. Somebody will say something, and I say, 'what's that?' And it's like, 'well, there's my new word of the day!'

Jeff built one career on having a nose for news and understanding the role of people in the story. When he came up with the idea for his business, he may not have looked like the perfect fit to lead it, but he let his curiosity, passion and vision guide him. Motivated to learn as much as possible as quickly as possible, he achieved a period of unforeseen personal growth.

Conversations about longer working lives typically have a pessimistic tone, but if you've designed a Work/Life Flywheel that creates consistent growth and momentum, why stop? Whatever stage of your career and life you are in, it never hurts to love what you do. And it's never too late to take on a new challenge.

How do we ensure we create a sustainable approach that enables us to make the consistent breakthroughs we need to feel like we're making progress? That's what we'll explore next.

───────────── **SUMMARY** ─────────────

- It's normal to experience crises of confidence and a lack of direction mid-career.
- To remind yourself of what matters, focus on what you look forward to most.
- Following your curiosity and concentrating on things that make you feel good helps you rediscover your purpose.
- Track your daily highlights to notice the things you enjoy doing every day, and do more of them!
- Curiosity is crucial because it's an opportunity to explore ideas without judgement.
- Being patient about seeing the results of your work is easier when you're doing something that aligns with your purpose and goals.
- It's never too late to reimagine your career, and there are always ways to deploy your skills and experience in new ways.

Breakthroughs

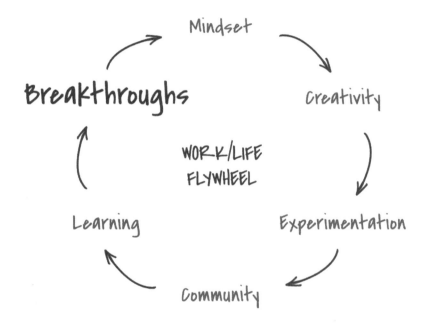

Mindset

Breakthroughs

Creativity

WORK/LIFE
FLYWHEEL

Learning

Experimentation

Community

19

Rest and recovery

Before Eliud Kipchoge attempted to break the two-hour marathon barrier in 2017, most experts and observers didn't consider the feat possible.

As it turned out, while he didn't manage it on that occasion (albeit running significantly faster than the official world record for the distance), he achieved the 'impossible' in Vienna two years later. Kipchoge's run shattered any notion that the time was beyond human capacity. However, it didn't enter the record books, primarily because of the rotating team of 35 pacemakers, seven of whom formed at all times a V-shape in front of Kipchoge to shield him from the wind. Ahead of them was a laser to guide them, and a pace car displaying the projected finish time based on their current speed.

Be in no doubt that Kipchoge is a remarkable athlete, combining incredible natural ability with the support of everything from Nike's development of ground-breaking running shoes to the very best nutrition experts. With such fine margins involved in elite running, though, he wouldn't have been able to run sub-two hours without the right pacing.

Anyone who has competed in any endurance activity will recognize the value of pacing yourself.

You don't complete a marathon by running flat out from the beginning. Instead, you carefully assess the distance and tailor your pace. First, ensuring you'll make it the whole way while giving yourself the best chance to complete the race in the lowest possible time. It's a delicate balance. Top athletes apply the concept of pacing to preparation as well as racing. Their whole training regime is a careful balance of strain and recovery, designed to give them the best opportunity to peak at particular points in a season, or in the case of the Olympics, over a four-year cycle. Get it wrong within a race, and you run the risk of what in cycling is rather bizarrely known as 'bonking' or, if you prefer, 'hitting the wall'.

Over a season, overwork can lead to peaking too soon and lacking the endurance to stay the course.

Consider how this relates to the world of work for a moment. If we were to design our ideal training regime, would it include staring into a screen for hours on end, day after day? Would we work flat out, every day, only taking the odd week off at random times throughout the year?

Nope.

PHYSICAL AND MENTAL ENDURANCE

Alex Hutchinson is an author and was formerly an elite long-distance runner for Canada's national team.

His book, *Endure: Mind, Body, and the Curiously Elastic Limits of Human Performance*,[41] explored not just Kipchoge's marathon record attempt but broader questions about how we train our bodies and minds to achieve peak performance. Importantly, in the context of this part of the Work/Life Flywheel, notice the choice of the word 'limits' in Alex's subtitle. Understanding the impact of rest and recovery on physical performance, he was keen to discover how we could measure their effects on our cognition.

To analyse this, let's return to the question about the effect of screens on our daily work with an anecdote that Alex shared when we spoke on the podcast.

Sports scientist Samuel Marcora is a leading expert on the link between physical and mental capacity in performance and has created a test for brain endurance training, which Alex too took to measure

---

[41] Alex Hutchinson, *Endure: Mind, Body, and the Curiously Elastic Limits of Human Performance*, HarperCollins, 2018.

its effect on his marathon training. Marcora's research suggests that consistent exposure to the experiment can help reduce mental fatigue and perception of effort, but I was more interested in asking Alex about the short-term effects.

Here's how he described it in his *Runner's World* article:

> For the next 60 minutes, my sole task is to keep my brain locked on [an] excruciatingly dull parade of shapes. They flash by rapidly, leaving no time to daydream, check the clock, or even glance out the window. Still, thoughts intrude. I wonder how hot it is outside, whether I should have started earlier... BZZZ. The screen turns red. The longer I continue, the more frequent my mistakes become. When the hour is finally up, I have that cotton-headed feeling of total mental exhaustion that's usually the cue to flop down in front of the TV for a few hours of mindless reruns.[42]

After several hours of concentrating on a screen flashing up a series of *Clockwork Orange*-style images, guess what? Alex was exhausted, and his physical and cognitive performance diminished. Sounds like a day of Zoom meetings to me!

From the perspective of high performance at work, we massively underestimate the value of pacing.

For many, there's little consideration of how to plan the best structure for the working day to optimize for the peaks, let alone a longer time horizon.

What might this look like in practice?

1. During the average week, you may need to prioritize key client presentations, write a new white paper or train a group of new recruits. Instead of just cramming these vital activities randomly into your calendar, plan around them.

2. Ensure you don't have hours of video calls throughout the day beforehand, and give yourself ample time just before the session starts to compose your thoughts and focus.

---

[42] www.runnersworld.com/training/a20795307/brain-endurance-training/

3. Allow time to balance these periods of intense work with more rest – perhaps even scheduling a holiday or a few days off immediately afterwards. While our work/lives aren't as predictable as the sporting calendar, most people can identify their busier times throughout the year in advance, so incorporate this into your planning.

Achieving peak performance requires thinking of yourself as an elite athlete, taking rest and recovery seriously.

MENTAL HEALTH

Talking of marathons, when I chatted with George Bettany to record our podcast interview, he'd just returned from Paris, where he had run his fourth marathon in the past two years.

George played football at a high standard throughout his youth but was eventually released from his professional contract at 19. However, he still looks at much of his work/life through the lens of an athlete. Not least, ensuring that everyone who works with him can see him prioritizing time for exercise and recovery in his calendar.

George is the co-founder of Sanctus, a mental health coaching company that achieved rapid growth during the COVID-19 pandemic. Alongside the usual pressures of an entrepreneur's work/life, George and his co-founders experience something unique. So many people outside the company recognize the impact they make on people's lives, they are willing them on from the sidelines. With that comes pride and motivation, but also pressure. How does he manage it? The advice he shares with me sounds simple but is crucial to succeeding in a 'creative endeavour' like entrepreneurship: Be Yourself.

To create, you have to express yourself. The values, the problem you're solving, the world you're trying to create. It's so personal because that's where the drive and the passion and the motivation come from. But then I've learned the hard way that I need to just be George. I am not Sanctus.

One significant benefit of outside support is the growing community of clients, partners, coaches and employees who have urged George and his team on through a period of rapid change.

However, the role of community in his work/life isn't exclusive to those involved with Sanctus. It was also his running pals who were the ones who encouraged him to take up marathons. After initially sharing some of his short daily training routes on fitness app Strava, other local folks messaged him, suggesting they make it a social run. Slowly, they developed some shared goals, which have steadily increased in difficulty. First, they took on a 5k, which soon doubled to 10k, then a half marathon before the entire 26.2 miles.

The discipline required to train for long-distance runs – combining consistent effort with rest and recuperation – has shaped his outlook on what it takes to perform at the highest level in business and influenced how he sets goals for himself, something which he'd got wrong in the past.

I've had such a breakthrough with this because I used to be so outcome-focused that it would crush me because I'd spend so much time in my head, I didn't perform at my best. I wanted the business to be a certain size. I wanted it to have a certain number of people, have a certain impact, and a certain amount of revenue. The marathon has completely changed that for me because I set the goal of running it in the best time I can, but accepted that I can't quite control it. I let go of the outcome, but it didn't mean I let go of the goal – the direction is clear. The experience completely flipped. I completed it, and it was so transformational. The only way I could describe it is that I'm lighter, more free, and I feel like I'm performing better.

THE POWER OF SLEEP

It's clear, therefore, that stepping away from the pressures of the urgent tasks at hand is an essential part of your work/life design, but what else do you need to consider?

Staying fit and healthy is one part of the puzzle, but make sure you take the time to recover from physical exertion too. An obvious but vital component of your recovery is sleep. While you can get away with a lack of sleep by switching it on for individual meetings and work interactions, it does leave you cognitively impaired, which increases the chances of making mistakes and producing lower quality work in the long run.

As Amie M. Gordon and Christopher M. Barnes wrote in a *Harvard Business Review* article:[43]

> Although our sleep tends to happen at home, we bring the consequences of poor sleep into the workplace, too. Leaders who report sleeping worse tend to engage in more abusive behaviors toward their employees (such as yelling at them in front of their colleagues) and have damaged relationships with those employees. Sleep-deprived leaders are also less charismatic and generally less effective in their leadership roles. Research indicates that overall, businesses benefit when employees are well-rested.

As someone who's been sleep deprived for most of the past decade, I rarely feel entirely well-rested. However, I've learned to adapt my behaviour to account for the worst of days.

During those periods where lack of sleep is unavoidable, try the following.

1. As far as possible, stick to more routine tasks, rather than those that require creativity and innovation, which are more vulnerable and likely to lead to poor decision-making.
2. Explain the situation to friends and colleagues. You don't need to bore them with it, but most people understand and are willing to help out and share the load – this is the sign of a great team; one that works together during great and more challenging times.
3. Lean on the advice of others to sanity-check your ideas.

---

[43] https://hbr.org/2020/03/how-working-parents-can-prioritize-sleep

Plus, while the amount of sleep you get is cumulatively important, you don't have to get it all in one go.

In his book *Wild Nights*,[44] Benjamin Reiss wrote:

> Sleep is both a universal need and a freely available resource for all societies and even species. So why is it the source of frustration for so many people today? Why do we spend so much time trying to manage it and medicate it, and training ourselves—and our children—how to do it correctly? And why do so many of us feel that, despite all our efforts to tame our sleep, it's fundamentally beyond our control?

He believes the issues result from our obsession with the concept of a 'good night's sleep', which conflicts with many people's natural circadian rhythms. Suddenly, when we don't get our 'eight hours', this creates anxiety, thus reducing our chances of sleeping well the next night – a vicious circle. The truth is, that the body is very resilient and can cope well with periods of little sleep. However, it's essential to allow yourself the time, where possible, to make a dent in that deficit.

All sounds good, but when you've got young kids, you rarely get enough sleep at night, however well planned.

What other options do we have?

MAKING UP FOR LOST SLEEP

Until two years ago, I had never been a napper.

But having introduced a daytime sleep into my life in 2020, it has been a lifesaver for me on too many occasions to count. While it can't replace the total number of hours lost at night, it gives me the boost I need to get through the afternoon productively. Or to stop me clinging on for dear life, at least.

How do I do it without feeling sluggish afterwards?

---

[44] Benjamin Reiss, *Wild Nights: How Taming Sleep Created Our Restless World*, Basic Books, 2017.

I follow Dan Pink's 'Nappuccino'[45] technique.

The trick to effective napping is to limit sleep to no less than 10 minutes and no more than 20. Timing it to coincide with my afternoon low point (which is generally seven hours after waking), I precede the nap with a coffee or cup of tea, which gives you a double-kick when you wake up since the caffeine takes around 25 minutes to kick in.

Lunch, Read, Coffee, Sleep, Wake, Bang, away we go!

WHY ARE WE STILL TALKING ABOUT SLEEP?

Since the amount and quality of your sleep impacts your mood, decision-making and, significantly, your creativity, you need to take this seriously.

As we've seen, uniquely human characteristics like creativity will become ever more critical in a future of work marked by ever more automation. How we think about problems and navigate our way through life will be more important than learning facts. Better sleep contributes to a better mood, which, neurologically, helps us consider less obvious solutions to challenging problems. Right before we arrive at an insight-led idea, there's heightened activity in our brain's anterior cingulate cortex (ACC), which, when activated, is the source of 'cross-connections'.

I can't pretend that I have the answer to a permanently positive mood or a perfect night's sleep, but let me share three triggers that will get your ACC kicking in:

1. A short *gratitude practice* of only five minutes releases dopamine and serotonin, significantly improving our mood.
2. *Physical exercise* releases dopamine and endorphins into your brain, leaving you feeling happier, more energetic, and with enhanced productivity.

---

[45] Daniel H. Pink, *When: The Scientific Secrets of Perfect Timing*, Canongate Books, 2018.

3. As well as the stress-relieving benefits *of getting outside and into nature*, it also helps with 'attention restoration', restoring depleted attention circuits, countering the effects of mental fatigue and burnout while fostering an open, meditative mindset.

For every two hours spent awake consuming new information and forming new memories, our brains should go 'offline' for an hour to process the thoughts. Yes, ideally, we'd get eight hours of sleep but we know life doesn't always go to plan.

So, if you're getting less than seven hours, like me, try some healthy hacking of your ACC.

FLOW AND RECOVERY

Continuing the theme of neurobiological triggers, let's return to flow for a moment.

While we've covered triggers extensively in Chapters 10 and 17, one thing we didn't mention is the four stages of the flow cycle:

- **Struggle**: When we initially immerse ourselves in a problem, taking on new information and pushing ourselves to discover more, it can feel tough. There are moments when it's difficult and you feel like you're not making progress. This is a good thing – keep pushing on.
- **Release**: When you really hit the wall and can't do any more, that's when you stop and step away from the problem entirely. Switching gears allows nitric oxide into our system, relieving us from the stress hormones – cortisol and norepinephrine – that build up during the struggle phase.
- **Flow**: Only when you return to the task at hand do you enter a flow state.
- **Recovery**: Being in flow takes a toll on the central nervous system and body, tapping into the energy and resources we build in preparation, so it's essential to step away afterwards and take some time to recover. If we want to experience flow's ongoing, long-term benefits, we need to allow these reserves to replenish. If not, injuries and burnout arise.

There's no glory in overwork and burnout.

To achieve major breakthroughs, take a leaf out of the sporting elite's book and begin incorporating pacing, active recovery and good sleep habits into your work/life.

As podcast guest Alex Soojung-Kim Pang neatly summarized:[46]

If you want rest, you have to take it. You have to resist the lure of busyness, make time for rest, take it seriously, and protect it from a world that is intent on stealing it.

SUMMARY

- Sustained high performance means pacing yourself.
- Plan your diary to balance intense periods with opportunities to stop and recover.
- Give yourself time throughout the working day to gather your thoughts and regain focus.
- Think like an elite athlete and consider how you manage your efforts to peak at the right times throughout the year.
- Being yourself and sticking to your values is vital to success and happiness.
- While setting goals is important, accepting that you can't control everything is liberating.
- Sleep is essential to recovery and high performance, so try to make up for lost hours through napping.
- If you're tired, you can offset the negative impacts with a gratitude practice, exercise and being in nature.
- Incorporate pacing, active recovery, and good sleep habits into your work/life to achieve your potential.

[46] Alex Soojung-Kim Pang, *Rest: Why You Get More Done When You Work Less*, Basic Books, 2016.

20

Moments of reflection

Nik Whitfield is a scientist, but he's also part philosopher. Two minutes into our first conversation, he spotted a picture of a constellation on the wall behind me, inspiring him to explain the concept of the 'double-slit experiment' in physics.

Apparently, back in the days of people like Einstein, Schrödinger and Dirac, quantum physics became accepted as a new model through which to look at the world or, more accurately, the universe. The double-slit experiment involves waves passing through two narrow, parallel slits to form an interference pattern of alternating dark and bright bands. Using this method, physicists discovered that the universe is only in a 'probable state' until you look at it, and *then* it decides what it is.

> This is crazy shit. This is nuts. Unfortunately, science hasn't really taken on board that the universe is not this objective thing that we look at. We are participating in it all the time. It is part of us, and we are part of it. It's like a bowl of soup. You are not a carrot in the soup. The carrot is soup. You might take the perspective of the carrot, but it's still soup. You can then change perspective and say I'm a potato in the soup, or now I'm all the soup, but you're still soup.

Who doesn't enjoy a philosophical metaphor involving food?!

Not that Nik would describe himself as a philosopher, by the way. Rather that, while he deals in logic and data, he has an open mind to new ways of doing things that have allowed him to grow a successful business and design a work/life that prioritizes joy and wellbeing.

It wasn't always that way.

EMPTYING THE STRESS BUCKET

For much of his early career, he did what young people often do – work hard and play hard.

After taking the step into founding a cyber security business in 2014, however, this kind of lifestyle was not sustainable. Worse, the stress and pressure of a fast-growing start-up were manifesting in severe back pain. So bad that he took to managing conference calls lying down. He was eventually told by a specialist that the only option was to have a metal shunt inserted into the cerebrospinal fluid in his spine.

That's when Nik decided he needed to take a different approach.

He'd been managing the pain with increasing amounts of painkillers, never addressing the root cause. He likens it to a red light on a car dashboard, which keeps flashing. It's no good turning off the flashing light without fixing the issue because it just stores bigger problems up for the future. In his case, he eventually realized that paying attention to the pain was the answer to solving it.

> I've learned that pain is the result of your stress bucket overflowing. If I don't take care of myself and pay attention to myself, then the bucket keeps filling up and overflows.

He began using body scan meditation and journaling. The meditation was his first acknowledgement of the physical pain. Journaling was a way of 'expunging it'. Recognizing that he'd experienced trauma in his life, he began journaling to write about the things he had buried inside him – anxiety, humiliation, anger, resentment, any kind of negative emotion.

After five years of medical interventions, including seeing countless specialists and taking up to 26 pills per day, within a month of implementing these new habits, 90% of the pain had gone.

His business has flourished in the years since, and has raised multiple rounds of venture capital to help scale its rapid growth. Most importantly for Nik, a positive approach to wellbeing is a fundamental part of the company's culture and has changed his life.

> It goes back to the analogy of your thought stream being a river. For most of my life, my head was in the river. I was in the thoughts. And so if I had a thought that the company might fail, then what's interesting is your body feels that. Even though it's not real and your mind just made it up, your body feels it. Sometimes the river would be rushing past, and it would be real turmoil, but practices like journaling, yoga and meditation helped me pull my head out. I suddenly realized, well, hang on, a lot of these thoughts are just pointless and unhelpful, so I'm just going to ignore those, whereas that one looks useful, so I'm going to pay attention to that.

By taking the time to reflect on the root causes of his pain, he has unlocked new levels of physical fitness and insight that feed directly into the success of his company and his happiness.

JOURNALING

While in Nik's case, journaling had an almost immediate, tangible impact – helping get rid of his back pain – it can deliver incredible results in a whole host of other ways too.

If there's one insight I can share with you based on hundreds of people I've interviewed and thousands I've surveyed over the past couple of years, it is that most people who describe themselves as 'happy' and 'fulfilled' practise some form of journaling. The effectiveness of journaling lies in reflection. We encounter vast amounts of information every day, and have countless sources of stimuli fighting for our attention and responsibilities stacked on top of each other. Pausing to reflect is crucial to allow our minds and bodies to recover.

Taking time to stop is also what separates smart, busy people from genius innovators. You can't achieve greatness without creating space to think.

Let's return to some great scientists to illustrate the point.

INNOVATION VS. INVENTION

When Albert Einstein searched for inspiration, he'd sail his boat into the centre of a lake and sit in solitude.

Away from the distraction of daily life, left alone to his thoughts, inspiration would strike. There's similar mythology around other inventors and thinkers. Leonardo da Vinci, for example, wrote his best ideas down backwards to avoid people plagiarizing his work. Thomas Edison used to leave his lab so rarely that once, after being awoken by a colleague from sleeping on his desk, he blurted out that he had better get home because he'd only that evening got married. Or so the story goes.

History-defining innovators touched with genius and whose methods are impossible to replicate.

Except there are two problems with the last sentence. First, I've deliberately confused invention and innovation. Secondly, the premise that there wasn't a method to the madness of these people assumes we can't impact our ability to innovate, which is entirely wrong.

Let me tell you why.

To be innovative is now up there with 'forward-thinking', being 'smart' and having 'integrity' when businesses talk about their culture and people.

As with any trope, these words have somewhat lost their meaning. I don't suppose many organizations would prioritize 'being stuck in the past', 'inept', or 'fast and loose with the truth'. Although, whether in the private or public sector or, indeed, in government, aspirations don't always align with reality.

Yet, in many respects, we've overplayed how innate is a talent for innovation.

Much like creativity, we seem to consider it something you're born with. The author Matt Ridley draws an important distinction between invention – 'coming up with a prototype of a new device or a new social practice' – and innovation – 'the business of turning a new device into something practical, affordable and reliable that people will want to use and acquire'. In *How Innovation Works*,[47] he explains that history has consistently demonstrated innovation happening slowly through testing and tweaking. It requires constant iteration and inevitable failure before you ultimately reach a breakthrough.

While 'a-ha' moments may come during periods in which we switch our brain off, as with the example of Einstein and his genius pals, by this point, the real work has already been done.

DESIGN THINKING

Sarah Stein Greenberg is Executive Director of Stanford University's Design School – known as 'the d.school'.

She and her colleagues teach the principles of design thinking, a process which now informs how some of the most brilliant businesses and organizations in the world innovate. They approach problems with a 'human-centric' view, making them more likely to develop realistic, actionable solutions.

Their methodology focuses on five stages:

- **Empathize**: Empathy allows you to set aside your assumptions and preconceptions to gain insight into the problem you're solving and for whom you're solving it.
- **Define**: After gathering your research, you define the problem from the user's point of view, e.g., 'We need to design a new model that empowers people to thrive and grow in work and life.'
- **Ideate**: When you're clear about the problem, you need to develop as many solutions as possible and start thinking about how you can test whether they'll be effective or not.

---

[47] Matt Ridley, *How Innovation Works*, Fourth Estate, 2020.

- **Prototype**: During this experimental phase, designers test their hypotheses in the real world. This may involve creating a physical prototype for a product, but it could equally apply to a new schedule, an approach to networking, or developing a content flywheel.
- **Test**: Although this is the final stage of the model, designers take an iterative approach, which requires testing, measuring results and then redefining the problem to start once again.

Like the Work/Life Flywheel, design thinking is not a linear process. For example, some insights from the test phase may mean learning something new about the user, allowing you to 're-empathize'. Or something may immediately inspire a new idea, taking you right back to the ideate phase.

The point is that you consciously design a new way of thinking that provides a platform to build something better.

FROM ACTION TO INACTION

What does the design thinking process have to do with reflection, you may be asking yourself.

Well, Sarah Stein Greenberg is very clear that alongside the importance of *action*, there's also a need for a certain amount of *inaction*, as she shared on Christopher Lochhead's *Follow Your Different* podcast:

> I think reflection is kind of the underappreciated partner of action. In a lot of cases, when people think about creativity, they think about brainstorming and exuberance and that spark of inspiration. But... it's like the peanut butter and jelly sandwich, those two things are inextricably linked: action and reflection.

She recommends a form of journaling to help inspire breakthroughs, using another framework created at the d.school, called 'What?/So What?/Now What?'

Here's how you might use it following a creative session:

- **What?** Write down everything that happened before reflecting on what it means.
- **So what?** Why is it important, and why did it feel like something you wanted to capture?
- **Now what?** What do you want to do about it? Is it something you can test, practise or improve upon?

Adopting a mindful approach to reflection is a critical aspect of how you learn, not least an understanding and awareness of *how* you think – what's known as 'metacognition'.

> (Metacognition) is one of those kinds of secret skills that I firmly believe should be embedded in the heart of our education. Learning *how* you learn... is so important because that's... how you can start to take control.[48]

I think you'll have gathered by now that innovation isn't about maverick inventors or boffins in lab coats.

It's about designing how we work to optimize for creativity and productivity. Yes, that's about providing the opportunity to collaborate with others, creating the conditions for focused work to get into flow, and constantly searching for new knowledge. However, it's also about creating moments for reflection every day.

High performance requires the energy to push yourself mentally and physically, so it's critical to counterbalance the exertion with downtime.

Of course, this is the part that we often forget, leading not just to exhaustion but also to diminished performance. In fact, it's worth contemplating for a moment why this is even more important when pursuing something we care about because, although it might sound strange, passion can lead to burnout. As *Future Work/Life* podcast guest

---

[48] *Follow Your Different* podcast.

Jennifer Moss explained in her book, *The Burnout Epidemic*,[49] some of the people most at risk of burnout are those who do work they 'love and feel passionately about', partly because this can create obsession rather than harmony. Remember, burnout doesn't necessarily mean breaking down. Its symptoms include:

- Feelings of energy depletion or exhaustion.
- Increased mental distance from one's job, or feelings of negativism or cynicism related to one's job.
- Reduced professional efficacy.

It can be hard to spot these signs when your head is 'in the river', which is why it's valuable having the support of your community – whether family, friends or collaborators – to look out for you. You might formalize this idea by building a 'challenge network', as author and organizational psychologist Adam Grant suggests in *Think Again*.[50] While Grant discusses using this to challenge your *thinking* – which is a great idea too, by the way – you can benefit from it in other aspects of your life too. Not least, looking out for your wellbeing with a nudge to slow down or take some time off.

The trick to building a sustainable approach to your creative and productive work/life is incorporating downtime into your schedule – not just hoping for moments of recovery and reflection but insisting upon it.

After all, why do you think it was that Einstein used to sail to the middle of that lake?

Now we've covered how to design your time to allow for reflection and recovery, let's consider how to track your progress.

---

[49] Jennifer Moss, *The Burnout Epidemic: The Rise of Chronic Stress and How We Can Fix It*, Harvard Business Review Press, 2021.
[50] Adam Grant, *Think Again: The Power of Knowing What You Don't Know*, W.H. Allen, 2021.

SUMMARY

- Ensuring that your 'stress bucket' doesn't overflow can help prevent physical and mental health challenges.
- Journaling is a powerful reflection tool, helping you manage and organize the vast amounts of information going through your mind every day.
- Innovation requires constant iteration and inevitable failure before you ultimately achieve breakthroughs.
- Design thinking takes a 'human-centric' view of problems to create realistic, actionable solutions.
- Reflection is a vital part of the creative and learning process.
- High performance requires the energy to push yourself mentally and physically, so it's critical to counterbalance the exertion with downtime.
- Passion can lead to burnout, so lean on your community's support and incorporate downtime in your schedule.

21

Tracking your progress

When I met Andy Ayim for the first time, I felt like we'd known each other for years.

Within a few minutes of the interview, he'd turned the tables and started asking *me* questions about my children and how I ended up writing my book. He then shared how it related to his own life. While it certainly helps that we've both lived in the same area of north London and shared similar recent experiences in our work/lives, our connection revealed something about Andy's personality. He's one of those rare people who combine curiosity and empathy to put anyone they meet at ease.

After an hour in his company, it's no surprise that despite only being in his mid-thirties, he has packed more into a decade than many of us do over a whole career, crowned by a recent MBE awarded to him by the Queen for services to diversity in the technology industry.

Growing up within the diverse and multicultural community of Tottenham, Andy developed his unique skills for building connections with people. When he tells me purpose drives him to help others achieve their potential, it doesn't carry that hollow sound that occasionally emanates from people trying to say the 'right thing'. He means it, and the evidence of how effective he is at meeting his objectives is clear when looking at his work with young entrepreneurs.

As an angel investor, he takes what he sees as his three key roles seriously:

1. Providing capital for people who can't easily access it.
2. Plugging knowledge gaps that deter and inhibit people from achieving success in early-stage ventures.
3. Giving access to his network of investors, mentors and supporters that aren't readily available to those outside of the 'traditional' backgrounds that dominate the start-up space.

FROM CONVENTIONAL TO TRANSFORMATIONAL

After taking a conventional route through university and on to a graduate role at a large corporate firm, Andy entered the tech industry and moved to Silicon Valley. Since then, he has carved out his niche by recognizing the things he's great at, that the world needs and is willing to pay for, and, most notably, that he loves. Then he doubled down on the areas in which he felt he could make the greatest impact – reducing the barriers for founders from unexpected places and backgrounds, to access funding and support.

Andy takes reflection seriously too and has developed a journaling habit that provides him with a unique level of self-awareness and insight.

Ever since he made the move to California and found himself swimming in new terminology and conventions, he has documented his thoughts and feelings every day in what he calls his 'tracker'. Alongside the blog he started writing to help 'translate the lingo for people back home in Tottenham', Andy has tracked his progress in his version of a digital journal, recording any significant events and emotions at the end of every day. He's able to use this not just as a tracking tool but also as a resource for new ideas as he regularly analyses the data to help him spot connections between patterns of behaviour and thinking. Through a combination of written notes and images – screenshots of messages or photos of memorable experiences – he has built up his 'second brain'.

Andy's tracker has trained him to pay more attention to the most significant events in his work/life, and crucially it has given him a simple way to monitor and observe his progress.

When you take a quick look at Andy's LinkedIn profile, you wonder how he juggles so many different roles and supports so many people in their careers, all while raising a young family. Yes, natural talent is one thing. However, just as key is the way he has embraced a creative mindset to build communities, with whom he shares *his* knowledge, but who also inspire him to continually learn. It's no wonder that he has achieved so many substantial breakthroughs so quickly.

Andy has built a perfectly functioning Work/Life Flywheel.

THE POWER OF PROGRESS

It's no coincidence that so many people looking to change careers describe themselves as stuck in a rut.

It's not even necessarily a sign that someone hasn't achieved success. After all, money and status can sometimes be the main obstacle to changing our work/lives – the so-called 'golden handcuffs'. As we get older and responsibilities stack up, a sense that we have fewer options can become stronger. If you have a mortgage to pay, multiple mouths to feed and an ever-increasing cost of living, it's impossible just to throw away all your inhibitions and blindly leap into a career move.

However, reimagining work needn't be a binary choice – either continuing in the same job, at the same employer, working the same hours, *or* quitting.

As we've seen through the stories of the many amazing people in this book, good things don't happen overnight. The secret is finding the motivation to get started and being consistent, while recognizing the progress you make on your journey. By understanding what matters to you, developing new habits that enable more creativity, experimentation and learning, and building your network, you're setting yourself up for success.

But you have to keep moving forward.

Teresa Amabile and Steven Kramer of Harvard Business School have done some fascinating work on the positive role of progress in our 'inner work lives'[51] – the internal emotions that reflect our day-to-day experiences.

They analysed the relative impact of progression and setbacks on the psychology of a wide variety of people in different job functions and seniority. In all cases, the single biggest influence on a sense of fulfilment in their role was a feeling of making progress. And while significant events like closing new client deals, winning awards, or successfully launching products positively impacted their feelings about their work, size of achievement was less important than you'd think.

Even small wins are enough to provide a tremendous positive boost to your 'inner work life'.

Unfortunately, our brains are wired to convey negative emotions even more powerfully than their positive counterparts, which is why we experience loss aversion – a tendency to prefer to avoid loss rather than acquire something new. Amabile and Kramer found that this is also true of our work/lives, overriding any positives by a factor of two.

This being the case, it's worth trying to reframe setbacks as learning opportunities and as necessary steps in supporting our progress.

For example:

- I didn't get the promotion I wanted, but now I understand what I need to improve on to be successful next time.
- We didn't win the deal, but from the feedback I've received, I know that we need to quantify the product's value better next time.
- The presentation didn't go to plan, and I know now that this type of role isn't for me, so I need to look for something that will bring me more joy.

Aside from mitigating the risks of negative emotions, how can we harness the positive, to create forward momentum?

---

[51] Teresa Amabile and Steven Kramer, *The Progress Principle: Using Small Wins to Ignite Joy, Engagement, and Creativity at Work*, Harvard Business Review Press, 2011.

Let's start by clarifying that the work you're doing doesn't need to change the world to be meaningful. It just needs to matter to you. This is why being clear about your values and goals in the first place makes a huge difference. Every time we complete a task or receive feedback that aligns with our purpose, however minor, we give ourselves something to cheer about. So, make sure you do it!

How?

MICRO-JOURNALING

Andy Ayim has created a relatively sophisticated journaling system that involves individually categorizing his reflections, making it easier to see connections. But you don't have to go this far. Like any part of your work/life, there's a danger of analysis paralysis – overthinking how or why you're doing something rather than focusing on getting it done.

So start small.

Micro-journaling is one habit that has changed my life over the past couple of years. At the end of each day, I spend five minutes noting down answers to the following questions:

1. How do I feel about the day in general – was it productive, frustrating, exciting, sad?
2. What's the main reason for feeling this way?
3. What was my biggest achievement at work?
4. What was my biggest achievement in my personal life.

I then do what I wrote about in Chapter 11 and what the author Matthew Dicks calls 'Homework for Life', noting down the answer to the question:

- What were the most story-worthy moments of the day?

The goal of an exercise like this is twofold – focusing your attention on the things that matter most and recognizing your progress each day. As we scrutinize what has happened during the day – however large or small – we acknowledge the significance of our work. We're placing a marker down by identifying a highlight that demonstrates our progress.

Five questions in five minutes, which have had the following five results for me:

1. **Reduced stress and anxiety**: Why? Taking a moment to pause helps me unwind before lying down to sleep.
2. **I can see I'm making progress**: It's easy to get caught on the treadmill of life, but tracking my highlights shows me how far I've come.
3. **I can spot patterns**: After a while, it's easy to see the activities and people that give you energy and those that suck it up. Do more of the good stuff!
4. **I see a positive connection between work and life**: I do better work when life is good. I'm a better dad, husband, and friend when work is good. I no longer dream of work/life balance. I design my work/life to work in harmony.
5. **My memory has improved, and time has slowed down**: I struggled to remember key events in my children's lives for years. Everything seemed to be flashing by. Now I have a memory log, can recall even the smallest moments, and I feel like I have more time to play with.

Breakthroughs keep your Work/Life Flywheel spinning in the right direction, but require rest, reflection and acknowledgement of your progress. So, to gain perspective and recognize your progress, take a step back from life's craziness and start tracking your achievements today.

SUMMARY

- Developing a journaling habit helps provide unique levels of self-awareness and insight.
- Recording significant events and emotions in a tracker allows you to spot connections between patterns of behaviour and thinking.
- As we get older and responsibilities rack up, a sense that we have fewer options gets stronger, but reimagining work needn't be a binary choice – either continuing in the same job or quitting.
- The secret is finding the motivation to get started and then giving yourself credit for the progress you make on your journey.
- Your work doesn't need to change the world to be meaningful. It just needs to matter to you.
- Micro-journaling focuses your attention on the things that matter most and recognizes your progress each day.

22

Trusting the process

My obsession with time has woven its way into every part of my life over the past ten years.

At work, I've been on a mission to maximize time and achieve more in fewer hours. At home, my wife and I are seemingly in a perpetual dance, manoeuvring our commitments around one another's, restricted by the seemingly exponential growth in the number of kids' activities and parties.

The thing is, I've been thinking about it wrong.

If we have 4,000 weeks on Earth – and I'll come back to why it's that number shortly – I'm coming up to halfway, and I've spent most of that time thinking about 'what's next?' and 'what does the future hold?' I'll tell my wife how much easier it will be when the children are through 'this tricky stage' during the more frustrating moments. As I mull over my latest work challenge, I'll project how 'if only I can get this done, the pieces will perfectly slot together'. But, of course, you can never anticipate what will happen next. As I look back at the previous few years, how much of what happened could I have predicted? Not very much at all.

Like you and so many others, I'm in the middle of a work/life transition.

Fundamentally reconsidering what to do and how to do it isn't easy. There are frequent moments of self-doubt. But it's OK to question your own decisions and fears for the future. Everyone does it, so the trick is to learn to 'trust the process'. To believe in your choices and recognize your progress every step of the way. While having a 'north star' can provide motivation and purpose, true satisfaction only comes if we recognize and enjoy the moment we're experiencing right now.

It's not just that we should trust the process. The process is all there is. The things that we do every day are all that matter.

Here's where I turn to Oliver Burkeman's wonderful book, *Four Thousand Weeks: Time Management for Mortals*.[52] For two decades, Burkeman's job was to write about productivity for *The Guardian* in a column entitled 'This Column Will Change Your Life'. After years attempting to extract value from every second of the day, you can understand that he'd have a complex relationship with time, which is why, I suppose, his thesis is so refreshing.

> To see if we can't discover, or recover, some ways of thinking about time that do justice to our real situation: to the outrageous brevity and shimmering possibilities of our four thousand weeks.

Burkeman explores the idea that the limited time we have isn't just something we have to manage, it's the defining feature of human life. He also puts into context the relative insignificance of all our lives when judged against human history. While we hear people talking about making an impact on the world, he explains, the reality is, they won't. Yet, Burkeman isn't attempting to depress us all with morbid pronouncements about the pointlessness of it all. Instead, he discusses that life is finite, only to emphasize that each choice we make affirms our priorities and sacrifices things of lesser importance. As he puts it, 'time management is all life is'.

Why am I getting so deep at this point of the book, you might be asking.

Well, despite giving you a model to follow, which will help you reimagine your work/life, I can't promise you that everything will go exactly to plan. Accepting that can be a relief, so try giving in to the fact

---

[52] Oliver Burkeman, *Four Thousand Weeks: Time Management for Mortals*, Bodley Head, 2021.

that there are some things you can't control and see how you feel. For example, you can rarely stick rigidly to the plan you create for yourself each morning, let alone predict your career trajectory and route, several years in advance. Rather than see this as a negative, consider how boring life would be if everything happened as predicted. And one thing is for sure, something unexpected will emerge, and new opportunities will arise that you would never previously have considered.

Yes, giving in to the power of time may seem like giving up, but actually, it's the opposite.

IT'S ALL ABOUT THE SMALL DECISIONS

It's liberating to accept that you can only influence what's happening in front of you now – the small decisions you make every day about how you prioritize your time. That's why developing the Work/Life Flywheel idea has been so important to me and has positively affected my life. Rather than chase the ideal of work/balance and constantly feel like I'm failing, I've learned to reframe my relationship with time.

By remaining open-minded and being clear about my purpose and goals, I recognize that I'm staying true to what matters to me, including relationships, health and things that bring me joy.

I've realized that life is more colourful and meaningful by embracing creativity and understanding the power of stories – my own and those of others.

At the mid-point of my life (or a little before, if all goes to plan), I finally understand that making progress demands trying new things, even when they don't work, and that's how real change happens.

Perhaps the most significant personal change is that I've grown to love meeting new people and, particularly, learning from them by following my curiosity.

And, as I write this, I'm the fittest I've ever been, physically and mentally, because I no longer compromise on looking after myself.

I've reimagined my career, but I haven't worked out all the answers, which is lucky as there's plenty more of my life to go. Through the examples I've shared with you and the stories of the wonderful people

I've written about, I hope you'll be inspired to redesign *your* work/life and take this unprecedented opportunity to grow.

In the meantime, trust the process, take care of yourself, and great work will flow.

SUMMARY

- Work/life transitions aren't easy, and you'll frequently experience moments of doubt.
- While having a 'north star' can provide motivation and purpose, true satisfaction only comes if we recognize and enjoy the moment.
- Accepting that not everything will go to plan can be a relief.
- There are some things you can't control, which is what makes life exciting.
- Focus on the small decisions you make every day.
- Rather than chase work/life balance, reframe your relationship with time and be open-minded.
- Concentrate on what really matters and what brings you joy.
- Embrace creativity and experimentation.
- Appreciate the pleasure of meeting new people, following your curiosity and constantly learning.
- Trust the process.

PART 3

WHAT'S NEXT?

Conclusion:
Sharing your ideas

Since that moment in 2020, when I started writing, my life has completely changed. My objective was never to become 'a writer', let alone a published author, but one thing led to another and here we are.

Alongside the incredible new connections and opportunities I've created over the past couple of years, writing has positively impacted my mental health, relationships and, as I wrote in Chapter 11, even my perception of time.

In its different forms – free-writing, journaling, micro-journaling, penning articles and producing newsletters – writing has influenced my work/life in five profound ways:

1. **Rediscovering my purpose and identity**: As I considered what to do next in life, writing helped me align what matters most, my unique skills, available opportunities and providing for my family.
2. **Defeating imposter syndrome**: Transitions are never easy, but simply writing down my feelings helps quieten my monkey mind and expunges self-doubt.
3. **Exploring new ideas**: During an intense learning period, free-writing and long-form articles expose things I don't yet clearly understand and consolidate my expertise.
4. **Creating a progress portfolio**: While it's easy to cringe or shake my head at something I've written about in the past,

documenting my work is the secret to successfully measuring and accelerating my progress.

5. **Slowing time**: Everyone experiences the feeling of time flashing by. I've built an external memory log by recording one key achievement and a story-worthy moment every day, meaning life no longer blurs into one.

If there's only one lesson I can share with you based on my experience, it's to put your ideas out there in the world.

Whether it's writing, podcasting or creating videos, expressing your thoughts in public is a catalyst for positive changes in your work/life. Once I got over my fear of doing so, it opened my eyes and countless doors.

On that note, I'm closing the door on this book, and going for a much-needed lie-down.

Acknowledgements

Eighteen months ago, I hadn't seriously contemplated writing a book. Yes, plenty of people had made the throwaway comment, 'you should write a book about that', over the years, but it wasn't a realistic proposition. Life was too hectic, and apparently, writing a book takes quite a lot of work.

Well, it turns out it *really is* a lot of work, and I wouldn't have been able to do it were it not for my wonderful wife, Carly. You've taught me a lot over the years, not least being bolder about the decisions I've made in my career, something that's possible because you're always there to support me. You always believed in me. Even during those periods when I started to wonder whether all the research, interviews and (very) early morning writing sessions were worthwhile, you kept pushing me on. Still, I'm sure you're glad it's done now! Until the next one, at least…

To my amazing children, Theo, Emmie and Asa, you've inspired me so much since you each arrived in my life and brighten every day. The older you get, the more I learn from you, and I hope that one day you'll be proud of the work that went into creating this book, even if it meant I was occasionally distracted and mentally exhausted by the process! I can't wait to see what you discover gives you meaning in life because whatever it is, I'm sure you'll do remarkable things.

Mum and Dad, thank you for everything you've done to help me get to where I am. I only ever remember you being supportive throughout every stage of my life and in whatever decision I made. That trust and confidence in me has had a huge impact, and it's a privilege knowing that whenever I need some words of advice and a pep talk, I just need to pick up the phone.

Dad, it's no coincidence that I've ended up writing a business book given our shared interests. As well as our conversations about everything from history and economics to politics and finance, I always loved following your lead and understanding what makes businesses and people tick. I'm fairly sure that there were some Jim Collins books on the shelves at home too, so perhaps the title was destined from an early age.

Mum, this book literally wouldn't be the same without your help. As my editor, proofreader, sense-checker and all-around biggest fan, you've had a massive impact on the end product. I don't know how many thousands of words you've reviewed over the past couple of years, but I'm certain that those that ended up here are better for having had you give them the once over. And sorry for swearing.

To my brother, James, I'm lucky that our lives have remained so interconnected and to have you backing me up whenever I need you. Who would have thought all those years ago that we'd be doing what we're doing now? Maybe all those hours playing Championship Manager did teach us something after all.

I'm lucky to have some brilliant friendships that I know will last a lifetime, so thanks to everyone who's heard me banging on about my book and the writing process over the past six months.

Ben, Ben and Rich – the Michelin crew who've given me a boost whenever I needed it, along with countless evenings of amusement. They might all blend into one, but they're always fun!

Keith, for the wide-ranging conversations and for putting me on to so many interesting new ideas over the years.

Rory, for the support from the beginning of my career pivot and for giving me feedback throughout.

Big thanks to Rick Nicholls for bringing my ideas to life with the book's illustrations.

A quick mention too for Cath Bishop, who was the person that initiated this project, suggesting I sign up for Alison Jones' 10-Day Business Book Proposal Challenge.

To Glenn Elliott, who gave me a perfectly timed glimpse into what a great book proposal looks like.

And, for that matter, thanks to Alison Jones for believing in the idea of the *Work/Life Flywheel* and steering me in the right direction along the way.

To everyone who contributed to this book, I really do appreciate you spending the time with me and sharing your stories. I wasn't able to include everyone's, but you all inspired me to make it to the end and produce something I hope will help others learn from your experience.

Finally, to all the people whose names I don't know. Those who've read the *Future Work/Life* newsletter over the past couple of years, tuned in to the podcast and are now reading this book. I hope that using the lessons and ideas I've shared helps you take this opportunity to reimagine your work/life and have a spectacular career.

Thanks again!
Ollie

Index